Debbie Bliss

ESSENTIAL
KNITS FOR KIDS

20 Fresh, New Looks for Children Two to Five

photography by Ulla Nyeman

TRAFALGAR SQUARE
North Pomfret, Vermont

knitting basics 8

downtime 36

special time 70

time out 106

classic cardigan 108

v-neck vest 112

anorak 116

hoodie 124

pencil case 130

satchel 132

scarf coat 136

knittingbasics

types of yarns

When choosing a yarn for children's hand knits it is important that you work with a fiber that is soft but also practical. Children are often more used to the lightweight freedom of fleeces, and they can be resistant to hand knits that they may consider scratchy and uncomfortable.

The yarns I have chosen for the designs in this book are either an extra fine merino or cashmere mixes. Although they create fabrics that are gentle against the skin, the other essential feature is that they are machine washable.

When knitting a garment always make the effort to buy the yarn specified in the pattern. All these designs have been created with a specific yarn in mind. A different yarn may not produce the same quality of fabric or have the same wash and wear properties. From an aesthetic point of view, the clarity of a subtle stitch pattern may be lost if a garment is knitted in an inferior yarn.

However, there may be occasions when a knitter needs to substitute a yarn—if the wearer has an allergy to wool, for example—and so the following is a guide to making the most informed choices.

Always buy a yarn that is the same weight as the one given in the pattern: replace a double knitting with a double knitting, for example, and check that the gauge of both yarns is the same.

Where you are substituting a different fiber, be aware of the design. A cable pattern knitted in cotton when worked in wool will pull in because of the greater elasticity of the yarn and so the fabric will become narrower; this will alter the proportions of the garment.

Check the yardage of the yarn. Yarns that weigh the same may have different lengths in the ball or hank, so you may need to buy more or less yarn.

Here are descriptions of my yarns and a guide to their weights and types:

Debbie Bliss Baby Cashmerino:
A lightweight yarn slightly lighter than a double-knitting yarn.
55% merino wool, 33% microfiber, 12% cashmere.
Approximately 137yd/50g ball.

Debbie Bliss Cashmerino Aran:
55% merino wool, 33% microfiber, 12% cashmere.
Approximately 99yd/50g ball.

Debbie Bliss Cashmerino DK:
55% merino wool, 33% microfiber, 12% cashmere.
Approximately 120yd/50g ball.

Debbie Bliss Rialto DK:
100% merino wool extra fine superwash.
Approximately 115yd/50g ball.

Debbie Bliss Rialto Aran:
100% merino wool extra fine superwash.
Approximately 87yd/50g ball.

buying yarn

The yarn label will carry all the essential information you need as to gauge, needle size, weight, and yardage. Importantly, it will also show the dye-lot number. Yarns are dyed in batches or lots, which can vary considerably. As your retailer may not have the same dye lot later on, buy all your yarn for a project at the same time. If you know that sometimes you use more yarn than that quoted in the pattern, buy extra. If it is not possible to buy all the yarn you need with the same dye lot number, use the different ones where it will not show as much, on a neck or border, as a change of dye lot across a main piece will most likely show.

It is also a good idea at the time of buying the yarn that you check the pattern and make sure that you already have the needles you will require. If not, buy them now as it will save a lot of frustration when you get home.

garment
care

Taking care of your hand knits is important because you want them to look good for as long as possible. Correct washing is particularly important for children's garments as they need to be washed often.

Check the yarn label for washing instructions to see whether the yarn is hand or machine washable, and if it is the latter, at what temperature it should be washed.

Most hand knits should be dried flat on an absorbent cloth, such as a towel, to soak up any moisture. Lying them flat in this way gives you an opportunity to pat the garment back into shape if it has become pulled around in the washing machine. Even if you are in a hurry, do not be tempted to dry your knits near a direct heat source, such as a radiator.

As children's garments are small, you may prefer to hand wash them. Use a washing agent that is specifically designed for knitwear since this will be kinder to the fabric. Use warm rather than hot and handle the garment gently without rubbing or wringing. Let the water out of the basin and then gently squeeze out the excess water. Do not lift out a water-logged knit as the weight of the water will pull it out of shape. You may need to remove more moisture by rolling in a towel. Dry flat as explained for machine washing.

techniques

cast on

slip knot

Your first step when beginning to knit is to work a foundation row called a cast-on. Without this row you cannot begin to knit.

There are several methods of casting on. You can choose a method to serve a particular purpose or because you feel comfortable with that particular technique. The two examples shown here are the ones I have found to be the most popular, the thumb and the cable methods.

In order to work a cast-on edge, you must first make a slip knot.

1 Wind the yarn around the fingers on your left hand to make a circle of yarn as shown above. With the knitting needle, pull a loop of the yarn attached to the ball through the yarn circle on your fingers.

2 Pull both ends of the yarn to tighten the slip knot on the knitting needle. You are now ready to begin, using either of the following cast-on techniques.

cast on

thumb cast-on

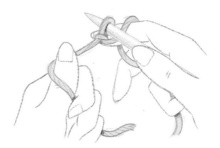

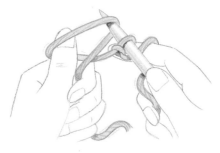

1 Make a slip knot as shown on page 13, leaving a long tail. With the slip knot on the needle in your right hand and the yarn that comes from the ball over your index finger, wrap the tail end of the yarn over your left thumb from front to back, holding the yarn in your palm with your fingers.

2 Insert the knitting needle upward through the yarn loop on your left thumb.

The thumb cast-on is a one needle method that produces a flexible edge, which makes it particularly useful for nonelastic yarns such as cotton. The "give" in it also makes it a good cast-on to use where the edge will turn back, as on the cuffs of the scarf coat (see page 136).

Unlike with two-needle methods, you are working toward the yarn end, which means you have to predict the length you need to cast on the required number of stitches. Otherwise you may find you do not have enough yarn to complete the last few stitches and have to start all over again. If unsure, always allow for more yarn than you think you need as you can use what is left over for sewing seams.

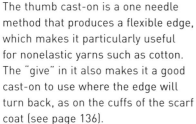

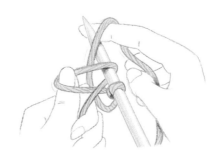

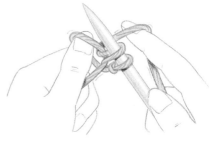

3 With the right index finger, wrap the yarn from the ball up and over the tip of the knitting needle.

4 Draw the yarn through the loop on your thumb to form a new stitch on the knitting needle. Then, let the yarn loop slip off your left thumb and pull the loose end to tighten up the stitch. Repeat these steps until the required number of stitches have been cast on.

cable cast-on

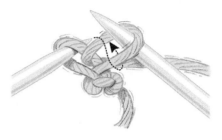

1 Make a slip knot as shown on page 13. Hold the knitting needle with the slip knot in your left hand and insert the right-hand needle from left to right and from front to back through the slip knot. Wrap the yarn from the ball up and over the tip of the right-hand needle as shown.

2 With the right-hand needle, draw a loop through the slip knot to make a new stitch. Do not drop the stitch from the left-hand needle, but instead slip the new stitch onto the left-hand needle as shown.

The cable cast-on method uses two needles and is particularly good for ribbed edges, as it provides a sturdy, but still elastic, edge. Because you need to insert the needle between the stitches and pull the yarn through to create another stitch, make sure that you do not make the new stitch too tight. The cable method is one of the most widely used cast-ons.

3 Next, insert the right-hand needle between the two stitches on the left-hand needle and wrap the yarn around the tip of the right-hand needle.

4 Pull the yarn through to make a new stitch, and then place the new stitch on the left-hand needle, as before. Repeat the last two steps until the required number of stitches have been cast on.

knit
&purl

The knit and purl stitches form the basis of almost all knitted fabrics. The knit stitch is the easiest to learn and is the first stitch you will create. When worked continuously it forms a reversible fabric called garter stitch. You can recognize garter stitch by the horizontal ridges formed at the top of the knitted loops.

After the knit stitch you will move onto the purl stitch. If you work the purl stitch continuously it forms the same fabric as garter stitch. However if you alternate the purl rows with knit rows it creates stockinette stitch, which is the most widely used knitted fabric.

knit

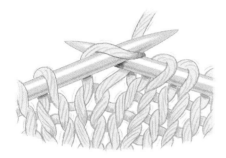

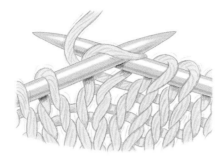

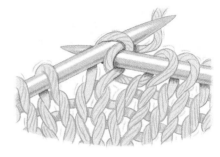

1 With the cast-on stitches on the needle in your left hand, insert the right-hand needle from left to right and from front to back through the first cast-on stitch.

2 Take the yarn from the ball on your index finger (the working yarn) around the tip of the right-hand needle.

3 Draw the right-hand needle and yarn through the stitch, thus forming a new stitch on the right-hand needle, and at the same time slip the original stitch off the left-hand needle. Repeat these steps until all the stitches from the left-hand needle have been worked. One knit row has now been completed.

purl

1 With the yarn at the front of the work, insert the right-hand needle from the right to the left into the front of the first stitch on the left-hand needle.

2 Then take the yarn from the ball on your index finger (the working yarn) around the tip of the right-hand needle.

3 Draw the right-hand needle and the yarn through the stitch, thus forming a new stitch on the right-hand needle, and at the same time slip the original stitch off the left-hand needle. Repeat these steps until all the stitches have been worked. One purl row has now been completed.

increase

increase one ("kfb")

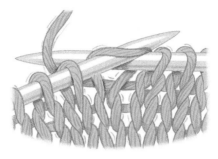 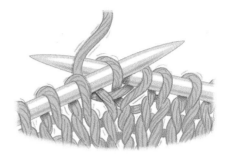

1 Insert the right-hand needle into the front of the next stitch, then knit the stitch but leave it on the left-hand needle.

2 Insert the right-hand needle into the back of the same stitch and knit it. Then slip the original stitch off the needle. Now you have made an extra stitch on the right-hand needle.

make one ("M1")

Increases are used to add to the width of the knitted fabric by creating more stitches. They are worked, for example, when shaping sleeves up the length of the arm or when additional stitches are needed after a ribbed border. Some increases are invisible, while others are worked away from the edge of the work and are meant to be seen in order to provide decorative detail. Most knitting patterns will tell you which type of increase to make.

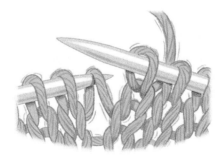 

1 Insert the left-hand needle from front to back under the horizontal strand between the stitch just worked on the right-hand needle and the first stitch on the left-hand needle.

2 Knit into the back of the loop to twist it, and to prevent a hole. Drop the strand from the left-hand needle. This forms a new stitch on the right-hand needle.

yarn over ("yo")

yarn over between knit stitches
Bring the yarn forward between
the two needles, from the back to
the front of the work. Taking the
yarn over the right-hand needle to
do so, knit the next stitch.

yarn over between purl stitches
Bring the yarn over the right-hand
needle to the back, then between the
two needles to the front. Then purl
the next stitch.

yarn over between a purl and a knit
Take the yarn from the front over
the right-hand needle to the back.
Then knit the next stitch.

yarn over between a knit and a purl
Bring the yarn forward between the
two needles from the back to the front
of the work, and take it over the top
of the right-hand needle to the back
again and then forward between the
needles. Then purl the next stitch.

bind off

Binding off is used to finish off your knitted piece so that the stitches don't unravel. It is also used to decrease more than one stitch at a time, such as when shaping armholes, neckbands, and buttonholes. It is important that a bind-off is firm but elastic, particularly when you are binding off around a neckband, to ensure that it can be pulled easily over the head. Unless told otherwise, bind off in the pattern used in the piece.

knit bind-off

1 Knit two stitches. Insert the left-hand needle into the first stitch knitted on the right-hand needle and lift this stitch over the second stitch and off the right-hand needle.

2 One stitch is now on the right-hand needle. Knit the next stitch. Repeat the first step until all the stitches have been bound off. Pull the yarn through the last stitch to fasten off.

purl bind-off

1 Purl two stitches. Insert the left-hand needle into the front of the first stitch worked on the right-hand needle and lift this stitch over the second stitch and off the right-hand needle.

2 One stitch is now on the right-hand needle. Purl the next stitch. Repeat the first step until all the stitches have been bound off. Pull the yarn through the last stitch to fasten off.

decrease

knit 2 together

knit 2 together ("k2tog" or "dec one")
On a knit row, insert the right-hand needle from left to right through the next two stitches on the left-hand needle and knit them together. One stitch has been decreased.

purl 2 together

purl 2 together ("p2tog" or "dec one")
On a purl row, insert the right-hand needle from right to left through the next two stitches on the left-hand needle. Then purl them together. One stitch has been decreased.

slip stitch over

Decreases are used to make the fabric narrower by getting rid of stitches on the needle. They are worked to make an opening for a neckline or shaping a sleeve cap. As with increases, they can be used to create decorative detail, often around a neck edge. Increases and decreases are used together to create lace patterns.

slip 1, knit 1, pass slipped stitch over ("psso")
1 Insert the right-hand needle into the next stitch on the left-hand needle and slip it onto the right-hand needle without knitting it. Knit the next stitch. Then insert the left-hand needle into the slipped stitch as shown.

2 With the left-hand needle, lift the slipped stitch over the knitted stitch as shown, and off the right-hand needle.

reading patterns

To those unfamiliar with knitting patterns they can appear to be written in a strange, alien language! However, as you become used to the terminology you will see that they have a logic and consistency that you will soon become familiar with.

Do not be too concerned if you read through a pattern first and are confused by parts of it because some instructions make more sense when your stitches are on the needle and you are at that point in the piece. However, it is sometimes a good idea to check with your local yarn store whether your skill levels are up to a particular design as this can prevent frustration later on.

Figures for larger sizes are given in parentheses ( ). Where only one figure appears, it means that this number applies to all sizes. Directions in brackets [ ] are to be worked as many times as instructed. Where a 0 (zero) appears, no stitches or rows are worked for this size.

When you follow the pattern, it is important that you consistently use the right stitches or rows for your size. Switching between sizes can be avoided by marking your size throughout with a highlighting pen on a photocopy of the pattern.

Before starting your project, check the size and the finished knitted measurements that are given for that size; you may want to make a smaller or larger garment depending on the proportions of the wearer it is intended for.

The quantities of yarn given in the instructions are based on the yarn

used by the knitter of the original garment and therefore all amounts should be considered approximate. For example, if that knitter has used almost all of the last ball, it may be that another knitter with a slightly different gauge has to break into another ball to complete the garment. A slight variation in gauge can therefore make the difference between using fewer or more balls than that stated in the pattern.

gauge

Every knitting pattern gives a gauge—the number of stitches and rows to 4 inches that should be obtained with the specified yarn, needle size, and stitch pattern. It is essential to check your gauge before starting your project. A slight variation can alter the proportions of the finished garment and the look of the fabric. A gauge that is too loose will produce an uneven and unstable fabric that can drop or lose its shape after washing, while one that is too tight can make a hard, inelastic fabric.

Making a gauge square

Use the same needles, yarn, and stitch pattern quoted in the gauge note in the pattern. Knit a sample at last 5 inches square to get the most accurate result. Smooth out the finished sample on

a flat surface, making sure you are not stretching it out.

To check the stitch gauge, place a tape measure or ruler horizontally on the sample and mark 4 inches with pins. Count the number of stitches between the pins. To check the row gauge, mark 4 inches with pins vertically and count the number of rows. If the number of stitches and rows is greater than specified in the pattern, your gauge is tighter and you should change to a larger needle size and make another gauge square. If there are fewer stitches and rows, your gauge is looser and you should try again on a smaller needle size. The stitch gauge is the most important to get right as the number of stitches in a pattern are set but the length is often calculated in measurement rather than in rows, and you may be able to work more or fewer rows.

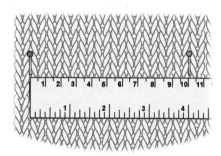

abbreviations

The following are the general knitting abbreviations used in this book. Any special abbreviations are given with the individual patterns.

standard abbreviations

alt = alternate

beg = begin(ning)

cont = continu(e)(ing)

dec = decreas(e)(ing)

DK = double knitting (a lightweight yarn)

foll = follow(s)(ing)

g = gram(s)

in = inch(es)

inc = increas(e)(ing)

k = knit

kfb = knit into front and back of next st

M1 = make one stitch by picking up the loop lying between the stitch just worked and the next stitch and working into the back of it

patt = pattern; or work in pattern

p = purl

psso = pass slipped stitch over

rem = remain(s)(ing)

rep = repeat(s)(ing)

skp = slip 1, knit 1, pass slipped stitch over

sl = slip

st(s) = stitch(es)

St st = stockinette stitch

tbl = through back of loop

tog = together

yd = yard(s)

yo = yarn over right-hand needle to make a new stitch (see page 19)

cables

back cross 6-stitch cable ("C6B")

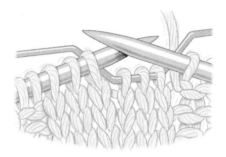 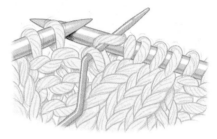

1 Slip the first three cable stitches purlwise off the left-hand needle and onto the cable needle. Leave the cable needle at the back of the work, then knit the next three stitches on the left-hand needle, keeping the yarn tight to prevent a gap from forming in the knitting.

2 Knit the three stitches directly from the cable needle, or if preferred, slip the three stitches from the cable needle back onto the left-hand needle and then knit them. This completes the cable cross.

front cross 6-stitch cable ("C6F")

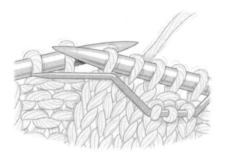 

1 Slip the first three cable stitches purlwise off the left-hand needle and onto the cable needle. Leave the cable needle at the front of the work, then knit the next three stitches on the left-hand needle, keeping the yarn tight to prevent a gap from forming in the knitting.

2 Knit the three stitches directly from the cable needle, or if preferred, slip the three stitches from the cable needle back onto the left-hand needle and then knit them. This completes the cable cross.

Cables are formed by the simple technique of crossing one set of stitches over another. Stitches are held on a cable needle (a short double-pointed needle) at the back or front of the work while the same amount of stitches is worked from the left-hand needle. Simple cables form a vertical twisted rope of stockinette stitch on a background of reverse stockinette stitch and tend to be worked over four or six stitches.

intarsia

Intarsia is used when you are working with larger areas of usually isolated color, such as when knitting large motifs. If the yarn not in use were stranded or woven into the wrong side, it could show through to the front or pull in the colorwork. In intarsia you use a separate strand or small ball of yarn for each color area and then twist the colors together where they meet to prevent a gap from forming.

vertical

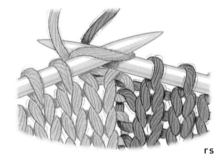

rs

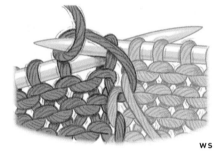

ws

changing colors on a vertical line
If the two color areas are forming a vertical line, to change colors on a knit row drop the color you were using. Pick up the new color and wrap it around the dropped color as shown, then continue with the new color. Twist the yarns together on knit and purl rows in this same way at vertical-line color changes.

right diagonal

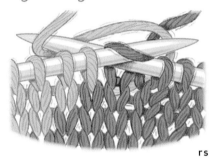

rs

ws

changing colors on a right diagonal
If the two color areas are forming a right diagonal line, on a knit row drop the color you were using. Pick up the new color and wrap it around the dropped color as shown, then continue with the new color. Twist the yarns together on knit rows only at right-diagonal color changes.

left diagonal

rs

ws

changing colors on a left diagonal
If the two color areas are forming a left diagonal line, on a purl row drop the color you were using. Pick up the new color and wrap it around the color just dropped as shown, then continue with the new color. Twist the yarns together on purl rows only at left-diagonal color changes.

reading charts

Most color patterns are worked from a chart rather than set out in the text. Each square represents a stitch and row, and the symbol or color within it will tell you which color to use. There will be a key listing the symbols used and the color they represent.

2nd size left front

2nd size right front

8 st patt rep

all sizes back, 1st and 3rd sizes left and right front

Unless stated otherwise, the first row of the chart is worked from right to left and represents the first right-side row of your knitting. The second chart row represents the second and wrong-side row and is read and worked from left to right.

If the color pattern is a repeated design, as in Fair Isle, the chart will tell you how many stitches are in each repeat. You will repeat these stitches as many times as is required. At each side of the repeat there may be edge stitches—these are only worked at the beginning and end of the rows and they indicate where you need to start and end for the piece you are knitting. Most color patterns are worked in stockinette stitch.

M pale pink   A mid green   B pale green

C ecru   D mid pink   E lemon   F chocolate

stranding

stranding on a knit row

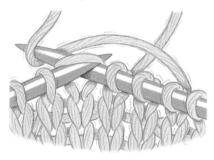 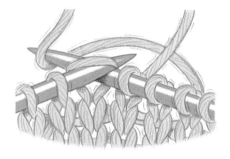

1 On a right-side (knit) row, to change colors drop the color you were using. Pick up the new color, take it over the top of the dropped color and start knitting with it.

2 To change back to the old color, drop the color you were knitting with. Pick up the old color, take it under the dropped color and knit to the next color change, and so on.

stranding on a purl row

Stranding is used when each of two colors is worked over a small number of stitches. The color you are not using is left hanging on the wrong side of the work and is then picked up when it is needed again. This creates strands at the back of the work called floats. Care must be taken not to pull the floats too tightly as this will pucker the fabric. By picking up the yarns over and under one another you will prevent them from tangling.

1 On a wrong-side (purl) row, to change colors drop the color you were using. Pick up the new color, take it over the top of the dropped color and start purling with it.

2 To change back to the old color, drop the color you were knitting with. Pick up the old color, take it under the dropped color and purl to the next color change, and so on.

&weaving in

weaving in on a knit row

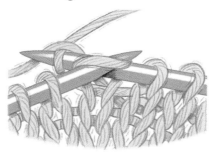 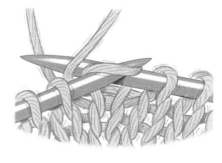

1 To weave in yarn on a knit stitch, insert the right-hand needle into the next stitch and lay the yarn to be woven in over the right-hand needle. Knit the stitch with the working yarn, taking it under the yarn not in use and making sure you do not catch this strand into the knitted stitch.

2 Knit the next stitch with the working yarn, taking it over the yarn being woven in. Continue like this, weaving the loose color over and under the working yarn alternately with each stitch until you need to use it again.

weaving in on a purl row

When there are more than four stitches between a color change, the floats are too long and this makes the fabric inflexible. You can also catch the long strands when wearing the garment, particularly on the inside of a sleeve. If you weave the yarn not in use into the wrong side, it is caught up before the next color change, thus shortening the float. Sometimes, depending on the color pattern, a combination of both stranding and weaving can be used.

1 To weave in yarn on a purl stitch, insert the right-hand needle into the next stitch and lay the yarn to be woven in over the right-hand needle. Purl the stitch with the working yarn, taking it under the yarn not in use and making sure you do not catch this strand into the purled stitch.

2 Purl the next stitch with the working yarn, taking it over the yarn being woven in. Continue like this, weaving the loose color over and under the working yarn alternately with each stitch until you need to use it again.

seams

When you have completed the pieces of your knitting, you reach one of the most important stages. The way you finish your project determines how good your finished garment will look. There are different seam techniques, but the best by far is mattress or ladder stitch, which creates an invisible seam. It can be used on stockinette stitch, ribbing, garter stitch, and seed stitch.

The seam that I use for almost all sewing up is mattress stitch, which produces a wonderful invisible seam. It works well in any yarn, and makes a completely straight seam, as the same amount is taken up on each side—this also means that the knitted pieces should not need to be pinned together first. It is always worked on the right side of the fabric and is particularly useful for sewing seams on stripes and Fair Isle.

I use other types of seams less frequently, but they do have their uses. For instance, backstitch can sometimes be useful for sewing in a sleeve cap, to neatly ease in the fullness. It is also good for catching in loose strands of yarn on colorwork seams, where there can be a lot of short ends along the selvage. Just remember when using backstitch for seams on your knitting that it is important to ensure that you work in a completely straight line.

The seam for joining two bound-off edges is handy for shoulder seams, while the seam for joining a bound-off edge with a side edge (selvage) is usually used when sewing a sleeve to the body on a dropped shoulder style.

It is best to leave a long tail end at the casting-on stage to use for seams, so that the seaming yarn is already secured in place. If this is not possible, when first securing the yarn for the seam, leave a length that can be darned in afterward. All seams on knitting should be sewn with a large blunt-ended yarn or tapestry needle to avoid splitting the yarn.

Before sewing side seams, sew the shoulder seams and sew on the sleeves, unless they are set-in sleeves. If there are any embellishments, such as applied pockets or embroidery, this is the time to sew them on, when you can lay the garment out flat.

seams

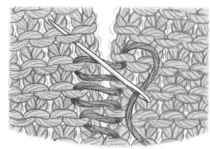

mattress stitch on stockinette stitch and double ribbing
With the right sides of the knitting facing you, insert the needle under the horizontal bar between the first stitch and next stitch. Then insert the needle under the same bar on the other piece. Continue to do this, pulling the thread through to form the seam.

mattress stitch on garter stitch
With the right sides of the knitting facing you, insert the needle through the bottom of the "knot" on the edge and then through the top of the corresponding "knot" on the opposite edge. Continue to do this from edge to edge, pulling the thread through to form a flat seam.

mattress stitch on seed stitch
With the right sides of the knitting facing you, insert the needle under the horizontal bar between the first and second stitches on one side and through the top of the "knot" on the edge of the opposite side.

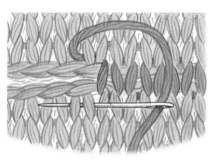

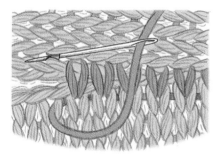

joining two bound-off edges (grafting)
1 With the bound-off edges butted together, bring the needle out in the center of the first stitch just below the bound-off edge on one piece. Insert the needle through the center of the first stitch on the other piece and out through the center of the next stitch.

2 Next, insert the needle through the center of the first stitch on first piece again and out through the center of the stitch next to it. Continue in this way until the seam is completed.

joining bound-off and selvage edges
Bring the needle back to front through the center of the first stitch on the bound-off edge. Then insert it under one or two horizontal strands between the first and second stitches on the selvage and back through the center of the same bound-off stitch. Continue in this way until the seam is completed.

picking up stitches

When you are adding a border to your garment, such as front bands or a neckband, you usually pick up stitches around the edge. A border can be sewn on afterward but this method is much neater. If you are picking up stitches along a long edge, a front band of a jacket for example, a long circular needle can be used so that you can fit all the stitches on. The pattern will usually tell you how many stitches to pick up.

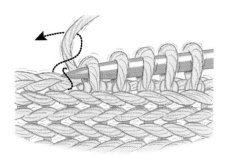

picking up stitches along a selvage
With the right side of the knitting facing, insert the knitting needle from front to back between the first and second stitches of the first row. Wrap the yarn around the needle and pull a loop through to a form a new stitch on the needle. Continue in this way along the edge of the knitting.

picking up stitches along a neck edge
On a neck edge, work along the straight edges as for a selvage. But along the curved edges, insert the needle through the center of the stitch below the shaping (to avoid large gaps) and pull a loop of yarn through to form a new stitch on the needle.

downtime

sizes and measurements

To fit ages 2–3 (3–4: 4–5) years

finished measurements

Chest 24 (26: 28)in

Length to shoulder 11$\frac{1}{2}$ (12$\frac{1}{2}$: 13$\frac{3}{4}$)in

Sleeve length 6$\frac{1}{4}$ (7$\frac{1}{2}$: 9)in

materials

4 (5: 6) x 1$\frac{3}{4}$oz/50g balls Debbie Bliss Baby Cashmerino in ecru

Pair each of sizes 2 and 3 knitting needles

gauge

25 sts and 34 rows to 4in square over St st using size 3 needles.

abbreviations

See page 23.

ballet top

back

With size 2 needles, cast on 69 (73: 77) sts.

K 5 rows.

Change to size 3 needles.

Beg with a k row, work 6 rows in St st.

Inc row K3, M1, k to last 3 sts, M1, k3.

Work 7 rows in St st.

Rep the last 8 rows 3 (4: 5) times more and the inc row again. 79 (85: 91) sts.

Work even until back measures 7 (8: 8$\frac{3}{4}$)in from cast-on edge, ending with a p row.

Shape armholes

Bind off 5 sts at beg of next 2 rows and 4 sts at beg of foll 2 rows. 61 (67: 73) sts.

Next row K3, skp, k to last 5 sts, k2tog, k3.

Next row P to end.

Rep the last 2 rows 2 (3: 4) times more. 55 (59: 63) sts.

Work even until back measures 11$\frac{1}{2}$ (12$\frac{1}{2}$: 13$\frac{3}{4}$)in from cast-on edge, ending with a p row.

Shape shoulders

Bind off 8 (8: 9) sts at beg of next 2 rows and 7 (8: 8) sts at beg of foll 2 rows.

Bind off rem 25 (27: 29) sts.

left front

With size 2 needles, cast on 59 (63: 67) sts.

K 5 rows.

Change to size 3 needles.

Next row K to end.

Next row K3, p to end.

Rep the last 2 rows twice more.

Inc row (right side) K3, M1, k to last 3 sts, M1, k3.

Work 7 rows as set.

Rep the last 8 rows 1 (2: 3) times more and the inc row once again. 65 (71: 77) sts.

Shape neck

Next row (wrong side) Bind off 9 sts, p to end. 56 (62: 68) sts.

Next row K to last 3 sts, k2tog, k1.

Next row P to end.

Rep the last 2 rows twice more. 53 (59: 65) sts.

Next row K3, M1, k to last 3 sts, k2tog, k1.

Next row P to end.

Cont in St st and dec 1 st at neck edge on every right-side row, **at the same time** work one more side-edge inc on the foll 7th row, then keep side edge straight and work until front measures 7 (8: 8³/₄)in from cast-on edge, ending with a p row.

Shape armhole

Next row (right side) Bind off 5 sts, k to last 3 sts, k2tog, k1.

Next row P to end.

Next row Bind off 4 sts, k to last 3 sts, k2tog, k1.

Next row P to end.

Next row K3, skp, k to last 3 sts, k2tog, k1.

Next row P to end.

Rep the last 2 rows 2 (3: 4) times more.

Keeping armhole edge straight, cont to dec 1 st at neck edge on every right-side row until 15 (16: 17) sts remain.

Work even until front measures same as Back to shoulder, ending at armhole edge.

Shape shoulder

Bind off 8 (8: 9) sts at beg of next row.

Work 1 row.

Bind off rem 7 (8: 8) sts.

right front

With size 2 needles, cast on 59 (63: 67) sts.

K 5 rows.

Change to size 3 needles.

Next row K to end.

Next row P to last 3 sts, k3.

Rep the last 2 rows twice more.

Inc row K3, M1, k to last 3 sts, M1, k3.

Work 7 rows as set.

Rep the last 8 rows 1 (2: 3) times more and the inc row once again. 65 (71: 77) sts.

Work 1 row.

Shape neck

Next row (right side) Bind off 9 sts, k to end. 56 (62: 68) sts.

Next row P to end.

Next row K1, skp, k to end.

Next row P to end.

Rep the last 2 rows once more. 54 (60: 66) sts.

Next row K1, skp, k to last 3 sts, M1, k3.

Next row P to end.

Cont in St st and dec 1 st at neck edge on every right-side row, **at the same time** work one more side-edge inc on the foll 7th row, then keep side edge straight and work until front measures 7 (8: 8¾)in from cast-on edge, ending with a k row.

Shape armhole

Next row (wrong side) Bind off 5 sts, p to end.

Next row K1, skp, k to end.

Next row Bind off 4 sts, p to end.

Next row K1, skp, k to last 5 sts, k2tog, k3.

Next row P to end.

Rep the last 2 rows 2 (3: 4) times more.

Keeping armhole edge straight, cont to dec 1 st at neck edge on every right-side row until 15 (16: 17) sts remain.

Work even until front measures same as Back to shoulder, ending at armhole edge.

Shape shoulder

Bind off 8 (8: 9) sts at beg of next row.

Work 1 row.

Bind off rem 7 (8: 8) sts.

sleeves

With size 2 needles, cast on 46 (50: 54) sts.

K 5 rows.

Change to size 3 needles.

Beg with a k row, work 4 rows in St st.

Inc row K3, M1, k to last 3 sts, M1, k3.

Work 5 rows.

Rep the last 6 rows 6 (7: 8) times more and the inc row again. 62 (68: 74) sts.

Work even until sleeve measures 6¼ (7½: 9)in from cast-on edge, ending with a p row.

Shape top of sleeve

Bind off 5 sts at beg of next 2 rows and 4 sts on foll 2 rows. 44 (50: 56) sts.

Next row K3, skp, k to last 5 sts, k2tog, k3.

Next row P to end.

Next row K to end.

Next row P to end.

Rep the last 4 rows 0 (1: 1) time more and then the first 2 rows 1 (0: 1) time. 40 (46: 50) sts.

Bind off.

front edging

Sew shoulder seams.
With right side facing and size 2 needles, pick up and k 9 sts from bound-off edge of right front, pick up and k 57 (63: 69) sts up right front neck, 25 (27: 29) sts from back neck, 57 (63: 69) sts down left front neck, then 9 sts from left front bound-off edge. 157 (171: 185) sts.
K 3 rows.
Bind-off row Bind off 3 sts, *slip st on right-hand needles back onto left-hand needle, cast on 2 sts onto left-hand needle, bind off 6 sts; rep from * to end.

ties (make 2)

With size 2 needles, cast on 125 (135: 145) sts.
K 3 rows. Bind off.

to finish

Sew sleeves into armholes, easing to fit. Sew side and sleeve seams, leaving a small opening in right side-seam level with beginning of neck shaping. Sew one tie to front edging on each front where neck shaping begins.

cozy sweater

● ● ● ● ● ● ● ● ● ● ▷

sizes and measurements

To fit ages 2–3 (3–4: 4–5) years

finished measurements

Chest $27^1/_2$ ($29^1/_2$: $31^1/_2$)in

Length to shoulder 15 ($16^1/_2$: 18)in

Sleeve length $8^1/_2$ ($9^3/_4$: 11)in

materials

6 (7: 8) x $1^3/_4$oz/50g balls Debbie Bliss Rialto Aran in lime (M)

1 (1: 1) x $1^3/_4$oz/50g ball Debbie Bliss Rialto Aran in stone (C)

Pair each of sizes 7 and 8 knitting needles

Set of size 7 double-pointed knitting needles

2 buttons

gauge

18 sts and 24 rows to 4in square over St st using size 8 needles.

abbreviations

See page 23.

back

With size 7 needles and C, cast on 66 (70: 74) sts.
K 1 row.
Change to M.
1st rib row (right side) K to end.
2nd rib row P2, [k2, p2] to end.
3rd rib row K2, [p2, k2] to end.
4th rib row P2, [k2, p2] to end.
K 4 rows.
Change to size 8 needles.
Beg with a k row, work in St st until back measures 8¾ (9: 9½)in from cast-on edge, ending with a p row.
Shape raglan armholes
Bind off 3 sts at beg of next 2 rows. 60 (64: 68) sts.
1st row K3, skp, k to last 5 sts, k2tog, k3.
2nd row P3, p2tog, p to last 5 sts, p2tog tbl, p3.
Rep the last 2 rows 5 times more. 36 (40: 44) sts.
Next row K3, skp, k to last 5 sts, k2tog, k3.
Next row P to end.**
Rep the last 2 rows until 22 (24: 26) sts rem, ending with a p row.
Leave these sts on a holder.

front

Work as given for Back to **.
Rep the last 2 rows 0 (1: 2) times more. 34 (36: 38) sts.
Next row (right side) Bind off 2 sts, skp, k to last 5 sts, k2tog, k3.
Next row P to end.
Next row K1, skp, k to last 5 sts, k2tog, k3.
Rep the last 2 rows until 20 (22: 24) sts rem, ending with a p row.
Leave these sts on a holder.

right sleeve

With size 7 needles and C, cast on 30 (34: 38) sts.
K 1 row.
Change to M.
1st rib row (right side) K to end.
2nd rib row P2, [k2, p2] to end.
3rd rib row K2, [p2, k2] to end.
4th rib row P2, [k2, p2] to end.
K 4 rows.
Change to size 8 needles.
Beg with a k row, work 4 (6: 8) rows in St st.
Inc row K3, M1, k to last 3 sts, M1, k3.
Beg with a p row, work 5 rows in St st.
Rep the last 6 rows 5 (6: 7) times more and the inc row again. 44 (50: 56) sts.
Work even until sleeve measures 8½ (9¾: 11)in from cast-on edge, ending with a p row.

Shape raglan sleeve top
Bind off 3 sts at beg of next 2 rows.*** 38 (44: 50) sts.
1st row K3, skp, k to last 5 sts, k2tog, k3.
2nd row P to end.
Rep the last 2 rows until 12 (16: 20) sts rem, ending with a p row.
Leave these sts on a holder.

left sleeve

Work as given for Right Sleeve to ***.
1st row K3, skp, k to last 5 sts, k2tog, k3.
2nd row P to end.
Rep the last 2 rows until 24 (28: 32) sts rem, ending with a p row.
Next row K3, skp, k to last 5 sts, k2tog, k3.
Next row Bind off 2 sts, p to end.
Next row P to end.
Next row K3, skp, k to last 3 sts, k2tog, k1.
Rep the last 2 rows until 10 (14: 18) sts rem, ending with a p row.
Leave these sts on a holder.

collar

With right side facing, size 7 needles, and M, k 19 (21: 23) sts from front holder, k last st of front tog with first st of right sleeve, k10 (14: 18), k last st of sleeve with first st of back, k9 (10: 11), k2tog, k9 (10: 11), k last st of back tog with first st of left sleeve, k9 (13: 17). 60 (72: 84) sts.
Next row K3, *p2, k2; rep from * to last 5 sts, p2, k3.
Next row P3, *k2, p2; rep from * to last 5 sts, k2, p3.
Rep the last 2 rows 7 times more and the 1st row again.
K 3 rows. Bind off.

button band

Sew right front and both back raglan seams. Sew left front raglan as far as bound-off sts.
With right side facing, size 7 double-pointed needles, and M, pick up and k 12 sts along left sleeve edge from start of collar to bound-off sts, break off yarn, then with right side of collar facing, a second double-pointed needle, and M, pick up and k 18 sts along edge of collar from start of collar to bound-off edge. 30 sts.
1st row (wrong side of collar, right side of sweater) P2, [k2, p2] to end.
2nd row K2, [p2, k2] to end.
3rd row Rep 1st row.
Change to C.
4th row P12, k18.
5th row K18, p12.
Bind-off row Bind off 12 sts purlwise, then 18 sts knitwise.

buttonhole band

With right side facing, size 7 double-pointed needles, and M, pick up and k 12 sts along left front edge to start of collar, break off yarn. With right side facing, a second double-pointed needle, and M, pick up and k 18 sts along edge of collar from bound-off edge to start of collar, break off yarn, then slip the 12 sts onto this needle. 30 sts.
Return to the top of collar and main ball of yarn.

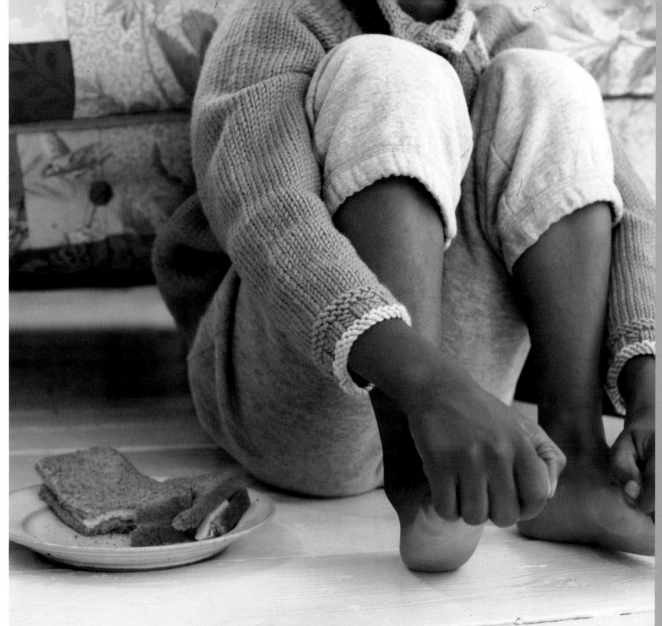

1st row (right side of collar, wrong side of sweater) P2, *k2, p2; rep from * to end.
2nd row K2, p2tog, yo, rib 6, p2tog, yo, rib to end.
3rd row Rep 1st row.
Change to C.
4th row K12, p18.
5th row P18, k12.
Bind-off row Bind off 12 sts knitwise, then 18 sts purlwise.

to finish

Sew side and sleeve seams. Lap buttonhole band over button band and sew in place. Sew on buttons.

measurements
Length approximately 41$\frac{1}{4}$in
Width approximately 41$\frac{1}{4}$in

materials
22 x 1$\frac{3}{4}$oz/50g balls Debbie Bliss Cashmerino Aran in each of chocolate (A) and raspberry (B)
Long size 8 circular knitting needle

gauge
18 sts and 30 rows to 4in square over seed st using size 8 needles.

abbreviations
See page 23.

note
Use a separate ball of yarn for each side edging, twisting yarns on wrong side to avoid a hole.

tv blanket

first side

With size 8 circular needle and A, cast on 181 sts.
Work back and forth in rows on circular needle as follows:
K 11 rows.
Foundation row With A, k5, with B, k to last 5 sts, with A, k5.
Patt row With A, k5, with B, k1, [p1, k1] 85 times, with A, k5.
Rep this row until blanket measures 40$\frac{1}{2}$in from cast-on edge, ending with a wrong-side row.
With A, k 11 rows.
Bind off.

second side

Work as given for first side, reading B for A and A for B.

to finish

Sew first and second sides together around the outer edge.

measurements
Approximately 10$\frac{1}{4}$in tall

materials
1 x 1$\frac{3}{4}$oz/50g ball Debbie Bliss Baby Cashmerino
in each of stone (A), white (B), jade (C), teal (D), and
rose (E)
Pair of size 2 knitting needles
Washable toy stuffing
$\frac{1}{2}$yd of narrow ribbon
1 small button

gauge
24 sts and 40 rows to 4in square over St st using
size 2 needles.

rag doll

53

abbreviations
s2togkp = slip next 2 sts tog knitwise, k1, then pass
slipped sts over so center st lies on top.
ssk = [sl 1 knitwise] twice, insert tip of left-hand
needle from left to right through fronts of slipped
sts and k2tog.
Also see page 23.

note
All pieces for the doll and dress are made using
size 2 needles.

The body is worked starting at the neck edge.

With A, cast on 17 sts.

P 1 row.

Inc row (right side) K4, M1, k1, M1, k7, M1, k1, M1, k4. 21 sts.

Work 3 rows in St st.

Inc row K5, M1, k1, M1, k9, M1, k1, M1, k5. 25 sts.

Work 3 rows in St st.

Inc row K6, M1, k1, M1, k11, M1, k1, M1, k6. 29 sts.

Work 13 rows in St st.

Change to B and k 2 rows.

Beg with a k row, work 8 rows in St st.

Shape crotch and legs

Next row Ssk, k12, ssk, k11, k2tog. 26 sts.

Next row P13, turn and work on these sts only for left leg, leave rem 13 sts on a spare needle.

Beg with a k row, work 5 rows in St st.

K 1 row.

Beg with a k row, work in striped St st of [4 rows C, 4 rows D] 5 times, then 2 rows in C.

Cont in D only.

Shape foot

Next row K4, cast on 10 sts, k9. 23 sts.

Work 3 rows in St st.

Next row K8, M1, k2, M1, k13. 25 sts.

P 1 row.

Next row K8, M1, k4, M1, k13. 27 sts.

Work 2 rows in St st.

Next row (wrong side) Bind off 13 sts knitwise, k to end.

Next row Bind off 10, k to end. 4 sts.

Sole

Next row [Kfb, k1] twice. 6 sts.

K 1 row.

Next row Kfb, k3, kfb, k1. 8 sts.

K 8 rows.

Next row K2tog, k4, ssk. 6 sts.

K 1 row.

Next row K2tog, k2, ssk.

Bind off rem 4 sts.

With wrong side facing and B, rejoin yarn to 13 sts on spare needle, p to end.

Beg with a k row, work 5 rows in St st.

K 1 row.

Beg with a k row, work in striped St st of [4 rows C, 4 rows D] 4 times, then 2 rows in C.

Cont in D only.

Shape foot

Next row K9, cast on 10 sts, k4. 23 sts.

Work 3 rows in St st.

Next row K13, M1, k2, M1, k8. 25 sts.
P 1 row.
Next row K13, M1, k4, M1, k8. 27 sts.
Work 2 rows in St st.
Next row (wrong side) Bind off 10 sts knitwise, k to end.
Next row Bind off 13, k to end. 4 sts.
Sole
Next row [Kfb, k1] twice.
K 1 row.
Next row Kfb, k3, kfb, k1. 8 sts.
K 8 rows.
Next row K2tog, k4, ssk. 6 sts.
K 1 row.
Next row K2tog, k2, ssk.
Bind off rem 4 sts.

arms (make 2)

The arm is worked from hand to shoulder
With A, cast on 5 sts.
P 1 row.
Next row K1, [M1, k1] 4 times. 9 sts.
P 1 row.
Next row K1, M1, k2, M1, k3, M1, k2, M1, k1. 13 sts.
Work 3 rows in St st.
Next row [K1, ssk] twice, [k1, k2tog] twice, k1. 9 sts.
Beg with a p row, work 13 rows in St st.
Next row Ssk, k5, k2tog. 7 sts.
P 1 row.
Next row Ssk, k3, k2tog. 5 sts.
P 1 row.
Next row Ssk, k1, k2tog. 3 sts.
P 1 row.
Next row S2togkp.

head

With A, cast on 9 sts.
Beg with a k row, work 2 rows in St st.
Next row K1, [M1, k1] 8 times. 17 sts.
P 1 row.
Next row [K2, M1] 4 times, k1, [M1, k2] 4 times. 25 sts.
P 1 row.
Next row K6, M1, k1, M1, k11, M1, k1, M1, k6. 29 sts.
Work 3 rows in St st.
Next row K7, M1, k1, M1, k13, M1, k1, M1, k7. 33 sts.
Work 5 rows in St st.
Next row K6, ssk, k1, k2tog, k11, ssk, k1, k2tog, k6. 29 sts.

hair

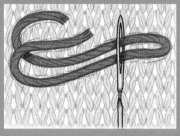

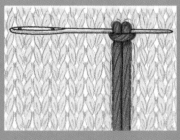

1 Thread a 5in loop of yarn through needle and insert point of the needle from top to bottom through bar in the center of a stitch or between two stitches.
2 Pull yarn loop through then remove needle. Pass the two yarn ends through the loop.
3 Place needle under the double yarn above the loop and pull yarn ends to tighten loop onto yarn.

Repeat these steps working hair all over head, working as densely or sparsely as required. Trim yarn lengths into a hair style.

Work 3 rows in St st.

Next row K5, ssk, k1, k2tog, k9, ssk, k1, k2tog, k5. 25 sts.

P 1 row.

Next row K2, [ssk, k1] twice, [ssk] twice, k1, [k2tog] twice, [k1, k2tog] twice, k2. 17 sts.

P 1 row.

Next row K2, [ssk, k1] twice, k1, [k1, k2tog] twice, k2. 13 sts.

P 1 row.

Next row K1, [ssk] twice, s2togkp, [k2tog] twice, k1. 7 sts.

Break off yarn, thread through rem sts, pull together, and secure.

to finish doll

Fold 10 cast-on sts of each foot in half and sew to form top of shoe. Sew leg and foot/shoe seams. Sew soles in place. Stuff feet/shoes and legs. Sew back and crotch seam, leaving cast-on edge open. Stuff body. Sew arm seams, leaving shaped top edge open. Stuff arms and sew to body using side shapings as a guide to position. Sew head seam. Sew head to neck edge. Attach lengths of yarn to head for hair strands (see hair steps opposite), and trim into your chosen style. Embroider a few stitches on face for eyes and mouth.

dress

With E, cast on 55 sts.

K 1 row.

Beg with a k row, work in St st until dress measures 3in ending with a p row.

Dec row K1, [k2tog, k1] to end. 37 sts.

K 4 rows.

Next row (wrong side) K8, bind off 3 sts knitwise, k until there are 15 sts on right-hand needle, bind off 3 sts knitwise, k to end.

Work on last group of 8 sts only for left back, leave rem groups of sts on a spare needle.

K 13 rows.

Bind off knitwise.

With right side facing, rejoin yarn to center group of 15 sts for front and k 3 rows.

Next row (wrong side) K5, p5, k5.

K 1 row.

Rep the last 2 rows twice more.

K 4 rows.

Bind off knitwise.

With right side facing, rejoin yarn to last group of 8 sts for right back and k 13 rows.

Bind off knitwise.

to finish dress

Sew 3 sts of left and right back to front for shoulders. Sew back seam from cast-on edge to beg of garter-st yoke. Make a small button loop on edge of left back and sew button on right back to match. Cut lengths of ribbon, thread through top of shoes, and tie in a bow.

measurements
Length 19in
Width 18in

materials
For one pillow
7 x 1³/₄oz/50g balls Debbie Bliss Rialto
Aran in pale blue (A) or mulberry (B)
1 x 1³/₄oz/50g ball in Debbie Bliss
Rialto Aran in mulberry (B) or pale
blue (A)
Pair of size 8 knitting needles

gauge
18 sts and 24 rows to 4in square over
St st using size 8 needles.

abbreviations
See page 23.

alphabetpillows

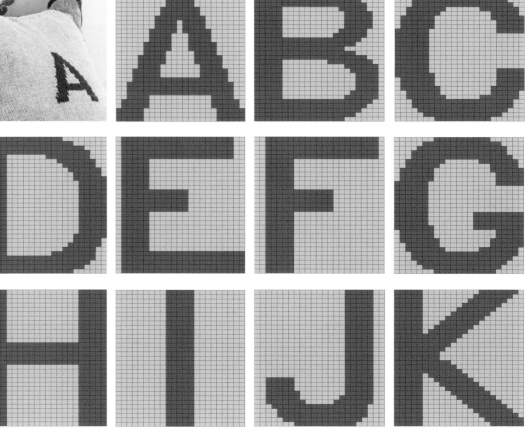

intarsia chart note

Use a separate small ball of yarn for each color area and twist yarns at color change to avoid holes forming. Read right side (k) rows of chart from right to left and wrong side (p) rows of chart from left to right, noting that 1st chart row is a wrong side (p) row.

A ▢   B ■   Each chart has 23 sts and 31 rows

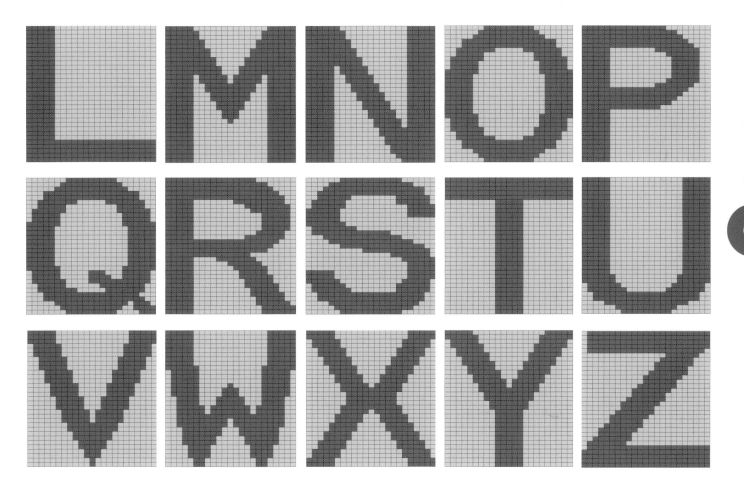

to make

With size 8 needles and A, cast on 83 sts.

Seed st row K1, [p1, k1] to end.

Rep the seed st row 5 times more.

Next row (right side) [K1, p1] 3 times, k71, [p1, k1] 3 times.

Next row [K1, p1] 3 times, p71, [p1, k1] 3 times.

Rep the last 2 rows 29 times more.

Seed st row K1, [p1, k1] to end.

Rep the seed st row 6 times more, so ending with a right-side row.

P 3 rows (the 2nd of these 3 rows forms the ridge row).

Seed st row K1, [p1, k1] to end.

Rep the seed st row 6 times more, so ending with a right-side row.

Next row [K1, p1] 3 times, p71, [p1, k1] 3 times.

Next row [K1, p1] 3 times, k71, [p1, k1] 3 times.

Rep the last 2 rows 16 times more, so ending with a right-side row.

Next row (wrong side) [K1, p1] 3 times, p24, p across 23 sts of 1st row of chart, p24, [p1, k1] 3 times.

Next row [K1, p1] 3 times, k24, k across 23 sts of 2nd row of chart, k24, [p1, k1] 3 times.

Rep the last 2 rows, working correct chart rows until chart is complete, so ending with a wrong-side row.

Next row [K1, p1] 3 times, k71, [p1, k1] 3 times.

Next row [K1, p1] 3 times, p71, [p1, k1] 3 times.

Rep the last 2 rows 15 times more, then the 1st of these 2 rows again.

Seed st row K1, [p1, k1] to end.

Rep the seed st row 6 times more, so ending with a right-side row.

P 3 rows (the 2nd of these 3 rows forms the ridge row).

Seed st row K1, [p1, k1] to end.

Rep the seed st row 6 times more, so ending with a right-side row.

Next row [K1, p1] 3 times, p71, [p1, k1] 3 times.

Next row [K1, p1] 3 times, k71, [p1, k1] 3 times.

Rep the last 2 rows 29 times more.

Seed st row K1, [p1, k1] to end.

Rep the seed st row 6 times more.

Bind off in seed st.

to finish

Lightly press, avoiding seed-st areas. Fold lower pillow back onto wrong side along ridge row and stitch back to pillow front along side edges. Fold upper pillow back onto wrong side along ridge row and stitch to pillow front along side edges, where it overlaps onto lower back, stitching through all thicknesses.

sizes and measurements
To fit ages 2–3 (3–4: 4–5) years
finished measurements
Chest 24 (26: 28)in
Length to shoulder 13 (14^1/$_2$: 16^1/$_4$)in

materials
6 (7: 7) x 1^3/$_4$oz/50g balls Debbie Bliss Rialto Aran in stone
Pair each of sizes 7 and 8 knitting needles
14 (16: 18)in open-ended zipper

gauge
18 sts and 24 rows to 4in square over St st using size 8 needles.

abbreviations
See page 23.

zipped vest

back

With size 7 needles, cast on 66 (70: 74) sts.
1st and 3rd sizes only
1st row (right side) P2, [k2, p2] to end.
2nd row P to end.
2nd size only
1st row (right side) K2, [p2, k2] to end.
2nd row P to end.
All sizes
Rep the last 2 rows 3 times more.
Change to size 8 needles.
Beg with a k row, work in St st until back measures 8^1/$_4$ (9^1/$_2$: 10^3/$_4$)in from cast-on edge, ending with a p row.
Shape armholes
Bind off 6 sts at beg of next 2 rows. 54 (58: 62) sts.
Cont in patt until work measures 13 (14^1/$_2$: 16^1/$_4$)in from cast-on edge, ending with a p row.
Shape shoulders
Bind off 15 (16: 17) sts at beg of next 2 rows.
Leave rem 24 (26: 28) sts on a spare needle.

left front

With size 7 needles, cast on 34 (36: 38) sts.

1st and 3rd sizes only

1st row (right side) P2, [k2, p2] to last 4 sts, k4.

2nd row K2, p to end.

2nd size only

1st row (right side) [K2, p2] to last 4 sts, k4.

2nd row K2, p to end.

All sizes

Rep the last 2 rows 3 times more.

Change to size 8 needles.

Next row (right side) K to end.

Next row K2, p to end.

These 2 rows form the St st with garter-st front edging.

Work even until front measures 8¹/₄ (9¹/₂: 10³/₄)in from cast-on edge, ending with a wrong-side row.

Shape armhole

Next row Bind off 6 sts, k to end. 28 (30: 32) sts.

Work even until front measures 11¹/₂ (13: 14¹/₂)in from cast-on edge, ending with a wrong-side row.

Shape neck

Next row (right side) K22 (23: 24) sts, turn and work on these sts only for first side of neck, leave rem 6 (7: 8) sts on a holder.

Dec 1 st at neck edge on next 7 rows. 15 (16: 17) sts.

Work even until front matches Back to shoulder, ending at armhole edge.

Shape shoulder

Bind off.

right front

With size 7 needles, cast on 34 (36: 38) sts.

1st and 3rd sizes only

1st row (right side) K4, p2, [k2, p2] to end.

2nd row P to last 2 sts, k2.

2nd size only

1st row (right side) K4, [p2, k2] to end.

2nd row P to last 2 sts, k2.

All sizes

Rep the last 2 rows 3 times more.

Change to size 8 needles.

Next row (right side) K to end.

Next row P to last 2 sts, k2.

These 2 rows form the St st with garter-st front edging.

Work even until front measures 8¹/₄ (9¹/₂: 10³/₄)in from cast-on edge, ending with a right-side row.

Shape armhole

Next row Bind off 6 sts, p to last 2 sts, k2. 28 (30: 32) sts.

Work even until front measures 11¹/₂ (13: 14¹/₂)in from cast-on edge, ending with a wrong-side row.

Shape neck

Next row (right side) K6 (7: 8) sts, slip these sts onto a holder, k to end. 22 (23: 24) sts.

Dec 1 st at neck edge on next 7 rows. 15 (16: 17) sts
Work even until front matches Back to shoulder shaping, ending at armhole edge.
Shape shoulder
Bind off.

collar

Sew shoulder seams.
With right side facing and size 7 needles, slip 6 (7: 8) sts from right front onto a needle, pick up and k 9 sts up right side of front neck, k 24 (26: 28) sts from back neck, pick up and k 9 sts down left side of front neck, then k 6 (7: 8) sts from left front holder. 54 (58: 62) sts.
1st rib row (wrong side) K2, p to last 2 sts, k2.
2nd rib row K4, [p2, k2] to last 6 sts, p2, k4.
These 2 rows form the patt and are repeated throughout.
Work 2¼ (2¾: 3)in more in patt, ending with a wrong-side row.
Next row (right side) K4, [p2, k2] to last 6 sts, p2, k4.
Next row K2, [p2, k2] to end.
Rep the last 2 rows until collar measures 4¾ (5½: 6¼)in, ending with a wrong-side row.
Bind off in rib.

armbands

With right side facing and size 7 needles, pick up and k 50 (54: 58) sts evenly along armhole edge.
1st rib row (wrong side) P to end.
2nd rib row K2, [p2, k2] to end.
Rep the last 2 rows 5 times more.
Next row P2, [k2, p2] to end.
Next row K2, [p2, k2] to end.
Rep the last 2 rows 4 times more and the first row again.
Bind off in rib.

pockets (make 4)

With size 7 needles, cast on 15 (17: 19) sts.
1st row (wrong side) K1, [p1, k1] to end.
2nd row Rep 1st row.
3rd row K1, p1, k11 (13: 15), p1, k1.
Rep the last row until pocket measures 2¾ (3¼: 3½)in from cast-on edge, ending with a wrong-side row.
1st buttonhole row K1, p1, k4 (5: 6), k2tog, yo, k5 (6: 7), p1, k1.
3rd row K1, p1, k(11: 13: 15), p1, k1.
Next row K1, *p1, k1; rep from * to end.
Rep the last row once more. Bind off in patt.

slim pocket
(make 1)

With size 7 needles, cast on 7 sts.
1st row (wrong side) K1, [p1, k1] to end.
2nd row Rep 1st row.
3rd row K1, p1, k3, p1, k1.
Rep the last row until pocket measures 4 (4½: 4¾)in from cast-on edge, ending with a wrong-side row.
Next row K1, [p1, k1] to end.

Rep the last row once more.
Bind off in patt.

to finish

Sew first 8 row-ends of armbands to sts bind-off at underarm. Sew side and armband seams, leaving last 8 rows of armbands unstitched. Fold armbands in half onto wrong side and slipstitch in place. Hand sew zipper in place behind front edging, from halfway along collar edge to cast-on edge. Fold collar in half onto wrong side and slipstitch in place. Sew on pockets. Sew on buttons.

special time

sizes and measurements

To fit ages 2–3 (3–4: 4–5) years

finished measurements

Chest 23^1/$_4$ (25^1/$_2$: 28)in

Length to shoulder 12^1/$_4$ (13^1/$_2$: 14^1/$_2$)in

Sleeve length 8^1/$_2$ (9^3/$_4$: 11)in

materials

5 (6: 6) x 1^3/$_4$oz/50g balls Debbie Bliss Baby Cashmerino in pale pink (M) and one ball in each of mid green (A), pale green (B), ecru (C), mid pink (D), lemon (E), and chocolate (F)

Pair each of sizes 2 and 3 knitting needles

3 buttons

60in of narrow ribbon

gauge

25 sts and 34 rows over St st and 27 sts and 34 rows over Fair Isle St st to 4in square both using size 3 needles.

fair isle jacket

back

With size 2 needles and M, cast on 101 (111: 121) sts.

K 3 rows. Change to size 3 needles.

Beg with a k row, work in St st until back measures 6^1/$_4$ (7^1/$_2$: 8^3/$_4$)in from cast-on edge, ending with a k row.

Dec row (wrong side) P2, [p2tog, p3] 19 (21: 23) times, p2tog, p2. 81 (89: 97) sts.

Now work in St st from Chart until back measures 7^1/$_2$ (8^1/$_4$: 9)in from cast-on edge, ending with a p row.

Shape armholes

Bind off 4 sts at beg of next 2 rows. 73 (81: 89) sts.

Dec 1 st at each end of next row and 3 (4: 5) foll right-side rows. 65 (71: 77) sts.

Work even until all 36 chart rows have been worked, then cont in M only until back measures 12^1/$_4$ (13^1/$_2$: 14^1/$_2$)in from cast-on edge, ending with a p row.

Shape shoulders

Bind off 13 (15: 17) sts at beg of next 2 rows.

Leave rem 39 (41: 43) sts on a holder.

left front

**With size 2 needles and M, cast on 51 (56: 61) sts.

K 3 rows. Change to size 3 needles.

Beg with a k row, work in St st until front measures 6^1/$_4$ (7^1/$_2$: 8^3/$_4$)in from cast-on edge, ending with a k row.

Dec row (wrong side) P2, [p2tog, p3] 9 (10: 11) times, p2tog, p2. 41 (45: 49) sts.**

Now work in St st from Chart until front measures 7¹/₂ (8¹/₄: 9)in from cast-on edge, ending with a p row.

Shape armhole

Bind off 4 sts at beg of next row. 37 (41: 45) sts.

Next row Patt to end.

Dec 1 st at beg of next row and 3 (4: 5) foll right-side rows. 33 (36: 39) sts.

Work even until front measures 9¹/₂ (10¹/₄: 11¹/₂)in from cast-on edge, ending with a p row.

Shape neck

Next row (right side) Patt to last 6 (7: 8) sts, leave these sts on a holder and cont on rem 27 (29: 31) sts.

Dec 1 st at neck edge on every row until 13 (15: 17) sts rem, **at the same time**, when all 36 chart rows have been worked, cont in M only until front measures same as Back to shoulder, ending at armhole edge.

Shape shoulder

Bind off.

right front

Work exactly as for Left Front from ** to **.

Now work in St st from Chart until front measures 7¹/₂ (8¹/₄: 9)in from cast-on edge, ending with a k row.

Shape armhole

Bind off 4 sts at beg of next row. 37 (41: 45) sts.

Dec 1 st at end of the next and 3 (4: 5) foll right-side rows. 33 (36: 39) sts.

Work even until front measures 9¹/₂ (10¹/₄: 11¹/₂)in from cast-on edge, ending with a p row.

Shape neck

Next row Patt 6 (7: 8) sts, leave these sts on a holder, patt to end and cont on rem 27 (29: 31) sts.

Dec 1 st at neck edge on every row until 13 (15: 17) sts rem, **at the same time**, when all 36 chart rows have been worked, cont in M only until front measures same as Back to shoulder, ending at armhole edge.

Shape shoulder

Bind off.

sleeves

With size 2 needles and M, cast on 41 (45: 49) sts.

K 3 rows.

Change to size 3 needles.

Beg with a k row, work 2 rows in St st.

Work Chart rows 33 to 36, as given for Left Front.

Cont in M only.

Inc 1 st at each end of next row and every foll 6th row until there are 61 (69: 75) sts.

Work even until sleeve measures 8¹/₂ (9³/₄: 11)in from cast-on edge, ending with a p row.

Shape top of sleeve

Bind off 4 sts at beg of next 2 rows. 53 (61: 67) sts.

Next row K2, skp, k to last 4 sts, k2tog, k2.

Next row P to end.

Rep the last 2 rows 3 (4: 5) times more. 45 (51: 55) sts.

Bind off 3 sts at beg of next 12 rows.

Bind off rem 9 (15: 19) sts.

2nd size left front
2nd size right front

8 st patt rep

all sizes back, 1st and 3rd sizes left and right front

| M pale pink | A mid green | B pale green | C ecru | D mid pink | E lemon | F chocolate |

neckband

With right side facing, size 2 needles, and M, slip 6 (7: 8) sts from right front neck holder onto a needle, pick up and k 24 (26: 26) sts up right front neck, k 39 (41: 43) sts from back neck holder, pick up and k 24 (26: 26) sts down left side of front neck, k 6 (7: 8) sts from left front holder. 99 (107: 111) sts.
K 3 rows.
Bind off.

button band

With right side facing, size 2 needles, and M, pick up and k 64 (68: 72) sts along left front edge.
K 3 rows.
Bind off.

buttonhole band

With right side facing, size 2 needles, and M, pick up and k 64 (68: 72) sts along right front edge.
K 1 row.
Buttonhole row K38 (40: 42), [k2tog, yo, k8 (9: 10)] twice, k2tog, yo, k4.
K 1 row. Bind off.

to finish

Sew sleeves into armholes, easing to fit. Sew side and sleeve seams. Sew on buttons. Thread ribbon through cardigan, just below beg of Fair Isle yoke.

sizes and measurements
To fit ages 2–3 (3–4: 4–5) years
finished measurements
Chest 12^1/$_4$ (15: 17^3/$_4$)in
Length to shoulder 6^3/$_4$ (7^1/$_2$: 8^1/$_4$)in
Sleeve length 6^3/$_4$ (7^1/$_2$: 8^1/$_4$)in

materials
3 (4: 4) x 1^3/$_4$oz/50g balls Debbie Bliss
Cashmerino Aran in jade
Pair each of sizes 7 and 8 knitting
needles

gauge
18 sts and 24 rows to 4in square over
St st using size 8 needles.

abbreviations
See page 23.

party shrug

left sleeve

With size 7 needles, cast on 34 (38: 42) sts.
K 3 rows.
Change to size 8 needles.
Beg with a k row, work in St st.
Work 2 rows.
Next row K3, M1, k to last 3 sts, M1, k3.
Work 5 rows.
Rep the last 6 rows until there are 46 (52: 58) sts.
Work even until sleeve measures $6^3/_4$ ($7^1/_2$: $8^1/_4$)in from cast-on edge, ending with a p row.**
Shape top of sleeve
Next row Cast on 4 (5: 6) sts, k to end.
Next row Cast on 4 (5: 6) sts, p to end. 54 (62: 70) sts
Next row K3, skp, k to end.
Next row P to last 5 sts, p2tog tbl, p3.
Rep the last 2 rows 10 (11: 12) times more. 32 (38: 44) sts.
Next row K3, skp, k to end.
Next row P to end.
Rep the last 2 rows 4 (6: 8) times more. 27 (31: 35) sts.
Work even for 6 (8: 10) rows.
Bind off.

right sleeve

Work as given for Left Sleeve to **.
Shape top
Next row Cast on 4 (5: 6) sts, k to end.
Next row Cast on 4 (5: 6) sts, p to end. 54 (62: 70) sts
Next row K to last 5 sts, k2tog, k3.
Next row P3, p2tog, p to end.
Rep the last 2 rows 10 (11: 12) times more. 32 (38: 44) sts.
Next row K to last 5 sts, k2tog, k3.
Next row P to end.
Rep the last 2 rows 4 (6: 8) times more. 27 (31: 35) sts.
Work even for 6 (8: 10) rows.
Bind off.

lower back border

Sew back seam.
With right side facing and size 7 needles, pick up and k 62 (66: 70) sts along row ends.
1st row P2, *k2, p2; rep from * to end.
2nd row K2, *p2, k2; rep from * to end.
Rep the last 2 rows twice more and the first row again.
Bind off in rib.

front and neck border

With right side facing and size 7 needles, pick up and k 35 (39: 43) sts along shaped edge, then 12 (16: 20) sts along straight row ends, then 35 (39: 43) sts along shaped edge. 82 (94: 106) sts.
1st row P2, *k2, p2; rep from * to end.

This row sets the rib.
Next 2 rows Rib to last 30 (36: 42) sts, turn.
Next 2 rows Rib to last 24 (28: 32) sts, turn.
Next 2 rows Rib to last 18 (20: 22) sts, turn.
Next 2 rows Rib to last 12 sts, turn.
Next 2 rows Rib to last 6 sts, turn.
Rib to end.
Work 5 more rows in rib across all sts.
Bind off loosely in rib.

to finish

Sew sleeve, side, and border seams.

polo shirt

sizes and measurements
To fit ages 2–3 (3–4: 4–5) years
finished measurements
Chest 27$\frac{1}{4}$ (29$\frac{1}{2}$: 32)in
Length to shoulder 13 (15: 17)in
Sleeve length 8$\frac{1}{2}$ (10: 11)in

materials
5 (6: 7) x 1$\frac{3}{4}$oz/50g balls Debbie Bliss Baby Cashmerino in black
Pair each of sizes 2 and 3 knitting needles
3 buttons

gauge
25 sts and 34 rows to 4in square over St st using size 3 needles.

abbreviations
See page 23.

back

With size 2 needles, cast on 88 (96: 104) sts.

1st rib row [K1, p1] to end.

This row forms the rib and is repeated.

Work 9 (11: 13) rows more in rib. Change to size 3 needles.

Beg with a k row, work in St st until back measures 8¼ (10: 11½)in from cast-on edge, ending with a p row.

Shape armholes

Bind off 6 (7: 8) sts at beg of next 2 rows. 76 (82: 88) sts.**

Next row K3, skp, k to last 5 sts, k2tog, k3.

Next row P to end.

Rep the last 2 rows 6 (7: 8) times more. 62 (66: 70) sts.

Work even until back measures 13 (15: 17)in from cast-on edge, ending with a p row.

Shape shoulders

Bind off 9 (9: 10) sts at beg of next 2 rows and 9 (10: 10) sts on foll 2 rows.

Bind off rem 26 (28: 30) sts.

front

Work as given for Back to **.

Divide for front opening

Next row (right side) K3, skp, k30 (33: 36), turn and work on these 34 (37: 40) sts only for first side of front neck, leave rem sts on a holder.

Next row P to end.

Next row K3, skp, k to end.

Rep the last 2 rows 5 (6: 7) times more. 28 (30: 32) sts.

Work even until front measures 11½ (13: 14½)in from cast-on edge, ending with a p row.

Shape neck

Next row K to last 7 (8: 9) sts, turn and work on these 21 (22: 23) sts only, leave rem 7 (8: 9) sts on a holder.

Dec 1 st at neck edge on next 3 rows. 18 (19: 20) sts.

Work even until front measures same as Back to shoulder, ending at armhole edge.

Shape shoulder

Bind off 9 (9: 10) sts at beg of next row. Work 1 row.

Bind off rem 9 (10: 10) sts.

With right side facing, join on yarn, bind off center 6 sts, k to last 5 sts, k2tog, k3.

Next row P to end.

Next row K to last 5 sts, k2tog, k3.

Rep the last 2 rows 5 (6: 7) times more. 28 (30: 32) sts.

Work even until front measures 11½ (13: 14½)in from cast-on edge, ending with a p row.

Shape neck

Next row K 7 (8: 9) sts, leave these sts on a holder, k to end. 21 (22: 23) sts.

Dec 1 st at neck edge on next 3 rows. 18 (19: 20) sts.

Work even until front measures same as Back to shoulder, ending at armhole edge.

Shape shoulder

Bind off 9 (9: 10) sts at beg of next row. Work 1 row.

Bind off rem 9 (10: 10) sts.

sleeves

With size 2 needles, cast on 50 (56: 62) sts.
1st rib row [K1, p1] to end.
This row forms the rib.
Work 15 rows more in rib.
Change to size 3 needles.
Beg with a k row, work 4 rows in St st.
Inc row K3, M1, k to last 3 sts, M1, k3.
Work 5 rows.
Rep the last 6 rows 7 (8: 9) times more and the inc row again. 68 (76: 84) sts.
Work even until sleeve measures 8½ (10: 11)in from cast-on edge, ending with a p row.
Shape top of sleeve
Bind off 6 (7: 8) sts at beg of next 2 rows. 56 (62: 68) sts.
Next row K3, skp, k to last 5 sts, k2tog, k3.
Next row P to end.
Rep the last 2 rows 6 (7: 8) times more. 42 (46: 50) sts.
Bind off.

button band

With right side facing and size 2 needles, pick up and k 27 (29: 31) sts evenly along right front edge to beg of neck shaping.
1st rib row K1, [p1, k1] to end.
2nd rib row P1, [k1, p1] to end.
Rep the last 2 rows 3 times more and the 1st row again.
Bind off in rib.

buttonhole band

With right side facing and size 2 needles, pick up and k 27 (29: 31) sts evenly along left front edge.
1st row K1, [p1, k1] to end.
2nd row P1, [k1, p1] to end.
Rep the last 2 rows once more.
Buttonhole row Rib 3, [yo, rib 2tog, rib 7 (8: 9)] twice, yo, rib 2tog, rib 4.
Rib 4 rows.
Bind off in rib.

collar

With size 2 needles cast on 39 (45: 51) sts.
Rib row K1, [p1, k1] to end.
Next row Cast on 6 sts, [p1, k1] 3 times across these sts, then rib to end.
Next row Cast on 6 sts, [k1, p1] 3 times across these sts, then rib to end.
Rep the last 2 rows 4 times more. 99 (105: 111) sts.
Change to size 3 needles.
Work even in rib until collar measures 3½in from cast-on edge.
Bind off in rib.

to finish

Sew sleeves into armholes easing to fit. Sew side and sleeve seams. Place lower edge of left front band over lower edge of right front band and sew in place. Starting and ending halfway across front bands, sew cast-on edge of collar to neck edge.

smock dress

sizes and measurements
To fit ages 2–3 (3–4: 4–5) years
finished measurements
Chest 25$\frac{1}{2}$ (28: 30$\frac{1}{4}$)in
Length to shoulder 19$\frac{3}{4}$ (22: 25$\frac{1}{2}$)in
Sleeve length 8$\frac{1}{2}$ (9$\frac{3}{4}$: 11)in

materials
7 (8: 9) x 1$\frac{3}{4}$oz/50g balls Debbie Bliss Baby Cashmerino in silver
Pair each of sizes 2 and 3 knitting needles
Size 2 circular knitting needle
4 buttons

gauge
25 sts and 34 rows to 4in square over St st using size 3 needles.

abbreviations
See page 23.

back

With size 2 needles, cast on 110 (120: 130) sts.

K 5 rows. Change to to size 3 needles.

Beg with a k row, work in St st until back measures 13³/₄ (15¹/₄: 17³/₄)in from cast-on edge, ending with a k row.

Dec row (wrong side) P2 (3: 4), [p2tog, p2] 26 (28: 30) times, p2tog, p2 (3: 4). 83 (91: 99) sts.**

Change to size 2 needles.

Work in garter st (k every row) until back measures 15 (17: 19³/₄)in from cast-on edge, ending with a wrong-side row.

Shape armholes

Bind off 5 (6: 7) sts at beg of next 2 rows. 73 (79: 85) sts.

Next row K2, skp, k to last 4 sts, k2tog, k2.

Next row K to end.

Rep the last 2 rows 7 (8: 9) times more. 57 (61: 65) sts rem.

Cont in garter st until back measures 19³/₄ (22: 25¹/₂)in from cast-on edge, ending with a wrong-side row.

Shape shoulders

Bind off 13 (14: 15) sts at the beg of next 2 rows. Bind off rem 31 (33: 35) sts.

front

Work as given for Back to **.

Change to size 2 needles.

Front opening

Next row (right side) K38 (42: 46), turn and cont on these sts only, leave rem sts on a holder.

Next row Cast on 7 sts, k these 7 sts, k to end. 45 (49: 53) sts.

Cont in garter st until front measures 15 (17: 19³/₄)in from cast-on edge, ending with a wrong-side row.

Shape armhole

Bind off 5 (6: 7) sts at beg of next row. 40 (43: 46) sts.

K 1 row.

Next row K2, skp, k to end.

Next row K to end.

Rep the last 2 rows 7 (8: 9) times more. 32 (34: 36) sts.

Cont in garter st until front measures 17³/₄ (19³/₄: 22³/₄)in from cast-on edge, ending with a right-side row.

Shape neck

Next row (wrong side) Bind off 13 (14: 15) sts, k to end.

Next row K to last 4 sts, k2tog, k2.

Next row K to end.

Rep the last 2 rows until 13 (14: 15) sts rem.

Work even until left front measures same as Back to shoulder shaping, ending at armhole edge.

Shape shoulder

Bind off.

Mark position for 2 buttons the first ³/₄ (1¹/₄: 1¹/₂)in above opening, the second ³/₄in below neck shaping.

With right side facing, rejoin yarn to rem 45 (49: 53) sts, k to end.

Cont in garter st until front measures 14¹/₂ (16¹/₂: 19¹/₄)in from cast-on edge, ending with a wrong-side row.

Buttonhole row K2, bind off 3 sts, k to end.

Next row K to end, casting on 3 sts over sts bound off in previous row.

Cont in garter st until front measures 15 (17: 19³/₄)in from cast-on edge, ending with a right-side row.

Shape armhole

Bind off 5 (6: 7) sts at beg of next row. 40 (43: 46) sts.

Next row K to last 4 sts, k2tog, k2.

Next row K to end.

Rep the last 2 rows 7 (8: 9) times more. 32 (34: 36) sts.

Work even in garter st, working 2nd buttonhole to match first when right front measures 17 (19: 22)in, then cont in garter st until right front measures 17³/₄ (19³/₄: 22³/₄)in from cast-on edge, ending with a wrong-side row.

Shape neck

Next row (right side) Bind off 13 (14: 15) sts, k to end.

K 1 row.

Next row K2, skp, k to end.

Next row K to end.

Rep the last 2 rows until 13 (14: 15) sts rem.

Work even until right front measures same as Back to shoulder shaping, ending at armhole edge.

Shape shoulder

Bind off.

sleeves

With size 2 needles, cast on 40 (44: 48) sts.

K 5 rows.

Change to size 3 needles

Beg with a k row, work in St st and inc 1 st at each end of the 5th row and every foll 6th row until there are 60 (68: 74) sts.

Work even until sleeve measures 8¹/₂ (9³/₄: 11)in from cast-on edge, ending with a p row.

Shape top of sleeve

Bind off 4 (5: 6) sts at beg of next 2 rows. 52 (58: 62) sts.

Next row K2, skp, k to last 4 sts, k2tog, k2.

Next row P to end.

Rep the last 2 rows 3 (4: 5) times more. 44 (48: 50) sts.

Bind off 3 sts at beg of next 12 rows.

Bind off rem 8 (12: 14) sts.

pockets

With size 3 needles, cast on 19 (23: 27) sts.

Beg with a k row work 3 (3¹/₂: 4)in in St st, ending with a k row.

Change to size 2 needles.

K 3 rows.

Buttonhole row (right side) K8 (10: 12), bind off 3 sts, k to end.

Next row K to end, casting on 3 sts over those bound off in previous row.

K 2 rows. Bind off.

to finish

Sew side and sleeve seams. Sew sleeves into armholes easing to fit. Sew on pockets. Sew on buttons.

● 92 striped tie

measurements
Length 8$^{1}/_{4}$in
Width 1$^{1}/_{2}$in

materials
1 x 1$^{3}/_{4}$oz/50g ball Debbie Bliss Cashmerino DK in each of black (A) and yellow (B)
Pair of size 6 knitting needles
12in (or neck size) of $^{1}/_{2}$in wide elastic
Small piece of black Velcro® hook-and-loop tape

gauge
22 st and 30 rows to 4in square over St st using size 6 needles.

abbreviations
ssk = [sl 1 knitwise] twice, insert tip of left-hand needle from left to right through fronts of slipped sts and k2tog.
Also see page 23.

● ● ● ● ● ● ● ● ● ● ● ● ▷

main section

With size 6 needles and A, cast on 18 sts.
Beg with a k row, work 3 rows in St st.
Beg with a p row, work 4 rows St st in B, then 4 rows in A.
Rep the last 8 rows 3 times more.
Work 4 rows in B.
P 1 row in A.
Dec row With A, k1, ssk, k to last 3 sts, k2tog, k1.
Rep the last 2 rows once more.
P 1 row in B.
Dec row With B, k1, ssk, k to last 3 sts, k2tog, k1. 12 sts.
Work 2 rows in B.
Beg with a p row, work 4 rows St st in A.
P 1 row in B.
Inc row With B, k2, M1, k to last 2 sts, M1, k2. 14 sts.
Work 2 rows in B.
P 1 row in A.
Inc row With A, k2, M1, k to last 2 sts, M1, k2. 16 sts.
Work 2 rows in A.
Work 4 rows in B.
Work 3 rows in A.
Dec row With A, k1, ssk, k to last 3 sts, k2tog, k1. 14 sts.
Work 3 rows in B.
Dec row With B, k1, ssk, k to last 3 sts, k2tog, k1. 12 sts.
Work 4 rows in A.
Work 3 rows in B.
Inc row With B, k2, M1, k to last 2 sts, M1, k2. 14 sts.
P 1 row in A.
Inc row With A, k2, M1, k to last 2 sts, M1, k2. 16 sts.
P 1 row in A.
Inc row With A, k2, M1, k to last 2 sts, M1, k2. 18 sts.
Beg with a p row, work 4 rows St st in B, then 4 rows in A.
Rep the last 8 rows 3 times more.
Work 4 rows in B.
Work 3 rows in A.
Bind off in A.

neck strip

With size 6 needles and A, cast on 9 sts.
Beg with a k row, work in St st until strip measures 3$\frac{1}{4}$in, ending with a p row. Bind off.

to finish

Fold main section in half lengthwise. Then taking a half stitch from each edge and matching stripes, sew seam using mattress stitch. Refold so that seam runs centrally and stitch across the ends. Sew neck strip in the same way, leaving ends open. Insert the elastic into the neck strip, so strip lies centrally and stitch to secure. Fold main section in half over the neck strip and stitch through all layers to form the "knot." Sew small pieces of Velcro® hook-and-loop tape to the ends of elastic.

beaded bag

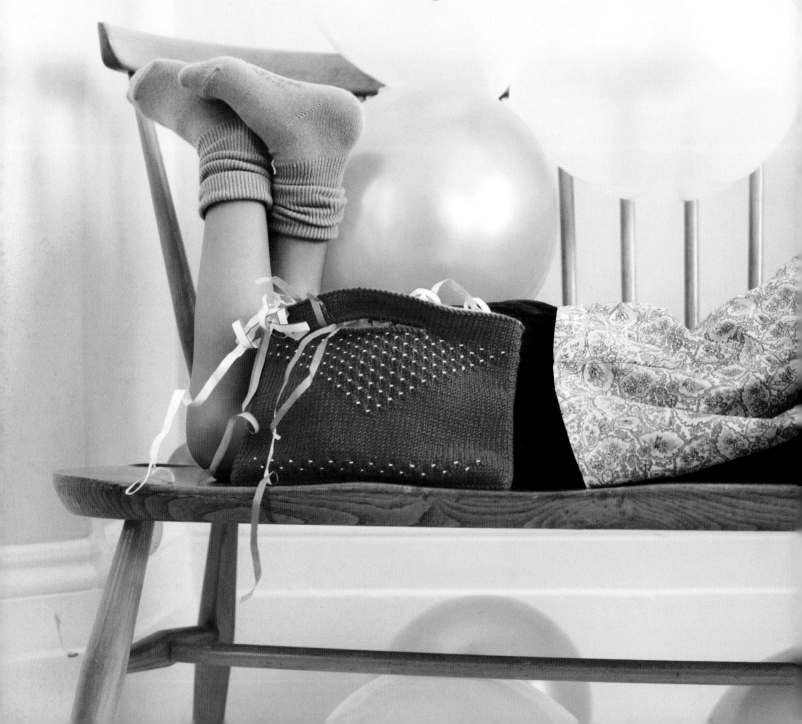

measurements
Height 6¹/₄in
Width 8³/₄in

materials
1 x 1³/₄oz/50g ball Debbie Bliss Baby Cashmerino in
old rose (A) and pale jade (B)
Pair of size 3 knitting needles
Approximately 260 small glass beads with a silver
core
Fine sewing needle and short length of sewing thread

gauge
25 st and 34 rows to 4in square over St st using size 3
needles.

abbreviations
b1 = bead one st by bringing yarn to front of work,
slide bead into position, p1, then take yarn to back of
work to k next st.
ssk = [sl 1 knitwise] twice, insert tip of left-hand needle
through fronts of slipped sts and k2tog.
Also see page 23.

note

The bag and lining are worked in one piece, from the base of the inner bag back, to the base of the inner bag front.

When buying beads, check that they have a central hole large enough for a double thickness of yarn to pass through.

You will need 256 beads for the bag. Thread beads onto yarn before starting, threading on a few more beads than are strictly necessary, in case of mistakes or damage. Remove damaged or misplaced beads on completion by breaking with a pair of pliers.

to make

Inner bag back

With size 3 needles and B, cast on 55 sts.

Beg with a k row, work 45 rows in St st, so ending with a k row.

Next row (wrong side) P17, bind off next 21 sts knitwise, p to end.

Next row K17, cast on 21 sts, k to end. 55 sts.

Beg with a p row, work 6 rows in St st.

Inc row P1, M1, p to last st, p1, k1. 57 sts.

Outer bag back

Change to A and k 1 row.

Ridge row (wrong side) K.

Beg with a k row, work 7 rows in St st.

Next row P18, bind off next 21 sts knitwise, p to end.

Next row K18, cast on 21 sts, k to end.

P 1 row.

Beg with a k row, work 47 rows from beading chart 1, so ending with a k row.

Base ridge row (wrong side) K.

Outer bag front

Beg with a k row, work 47 rows from beading chart 2, so ending with a k row.

P 1 row.

Next row K18, bind off next 21 sts purlwise, k to end.

Next row P18, cast on 21 sts, p to end.

Beg with a k row, work 7 rows in St st.

Ridge row (wrong side) K.

Inner bag front

Change to B.

Dec row Ssk, k to last 2 sts, k2tog. 55 sts.

Beg with a p row, work 6 rows in St st.

Next row (wrong side) P17, bind off next 21 sts knitwise, p to end.

Next row K17, cast on 21 sts, k to end.

Beg with a p row, work 45 rows in St st, so ending with a p row.

Bind off.

to finish

Sew together cast-on and bound-off edges to form base of inner bag. Sew together inner bag edges. Fold outer bag along base ridge row, sew together sides of outer bag, then slipstitch inner to outer bag around edges of handle openings.

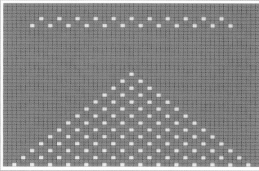
chart 1

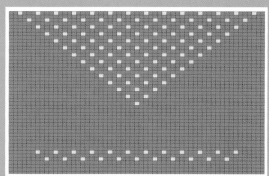
chart 2

☐ b1 (bead one stitch—see abbreviations for full explanation)

peacoat

sizes and measurements
To fit ages 2–3 (3–4: 4–5) years
finished measurements
Chest 30³/₄ (32³/₄: 34¹/₄)in
Length to shoulder 15³/₄ (17¹/₄: 19)in
Sleeve length with cuff turned back 9¹/₂ (10³/₄: 11³/₄)in

materials
9 (10: 11) x 1³/₄oz/50g balls Debbie Bliss Rialto Aran in stone (M)
1 (1: 1) x 1³/₄oz/50g ball Debbie Bliss Rialto Aran in navy (C)
Pair each of sizes 7 and 8 knitting needles
Set of size 7 double-pointed knitting needles
6 buttons

gauge
18 sts and 30 rows to 4in square over seed st using size 8 needles.

abbreviations
See page 23.

back

With size 7 needles and C, cast on 71 (75: 79) sts.

K 1 row.

Change to size 8 needles and cont in M only.

Next row (right side) K to end.

Seed st row K1, [p1, k1] to end.

This row forms the seed st.

Cont in seed st until back measures 10³/₄ (11³/₄: 13)in from cast-on edge, ending with a wrong-side row.

Shape armholes

Bind off 6 sts at beg of next 2 rows. 59 (63: 67) sts.

Work even until back measures 15³/₄ (17¹/₄: 19)in from cast-on edge, ending with a wrong-side row.

Shape shoulders

Bind off 10 (10: 11) sts at beg of next 2 rows and 9 (10: 10) sts at beg of foll 2 rows.

Bind off rem 21 (23: 25) sts.

right front

With size 7 needles and C, cast on 45 (47: 49) sts.

K 1 row.

Change to size 8 needles and cont in M only.

Next row (right side) K to end.

Seed st row P1, [k1, p1] to end.

This row forms the seed st.

Cont in seed st until front measures 10³/₄ (11³/₄: 13)in from cast-on edge, ending with a right-side row.

Shape armhole

Bind off 6 sts at beg of next row. 39 (41: 43) sts.

Work even until front measures 13³/₄ (15¹/₄: 17)in from cast-on edge, ending with a wrong-side row.

Shape neck

Next row Bind off 15 (16: 17) sts, seed st to end. 24 (25: 26) sts.

Dec 1 st at neck edge on every row until 19 (20: 21) sts rem.

Work even until front matches Back to shoulder, ending at side edge.

Shape shoulder

Bind off 10 (10: 11) sts at beg of next row.

Work 1 row.

Bind off rem 9 (10: 10) sts.

Place markers for 3 pairs of buttons; the first pair 6 (6³/₄: 7¹/₂)in from cast-on edge, the third pair 4 (4¹/₄: 4³/₄)in from neck edge and the remaining pair spaced halfway between.

left front

With size 7 needles and C, cast on 45 (47: 49) sts.

K 1 row.

Change to size 8 needles and cont in M only.

Next row (right side) K to end.

Seed st row P1, [k1, p1] to end.

This row forms the seed st.

Work as given for Right Front, reversing all shapings and working buttonholes to match markers as follows:

Buttonhole row (right side) Seed st 25 (26: 27), work 2 tog, yo, seed st 14 (15: 16), yo, p2tog, k1, p1.

collar

Sew shoulder seams.
With wrong side facing, size 7 needles, and M, miss the first 12 (13: 14) bound-off sts of left front neck then pick up and k 3 sts from rem bound-off sts, 13 (14: 15) sts up left side of front neck, 21 (23: 25) sts across back neck, 13 (14: 15) sts down right side of right front neck, then 3 sts from the first 3 right front neck bound-off sts. 53 (57: 61) sts.
Next row (right side) K1, [p1, k1] to end.
This row forms the seed st and is repeated.
Next 2 rows Patt to last 14 sts, turn.
Next 2 rows Patt to last 11 sts, turn.
Next 2 rows Patt to last 8 sts, turn.
Next 2 rows Patt to last 5 sts, turn.
Next row Patt to end.
Cont in patt and work 2¼ (2¼: 2¾)in more across all sts, ending with a wrong-side row.
Break off M.
With right side of collar facing, size 7 double-pointed needle, and C, pick up and k 17 (17: 19) sts along row ends of collar, k across 53 (57: 61) sts on needle, then with a second size 7 double-pointed needle, pick up and k 17 (17: 19) sts along row ends of collar. 87 (91: 99) sts.
K 1 row. Bind off.

sleeves

With size 7 needles and C, cast on 31 (33: 35) sts.
K 1 row.
Change to size 8 needles and cont in M only.
Next row (right side) K to end.
Seed st row P1, *k1, p1; rep from * to end.
This row forms the seed st and is repeated.
Work 11 (13: 15) rows more and place markers at each end of last row.
Change to size 7 needles.
Work 12 (14: 16) rows more.
Change to size 8 needles.
Inc and work into seed st one st at each end of the next row and every foll 6th row until there are 47 (51: 57) sts.
Work even until sleeve measures 9½ (10¾: 11¾)in from markers, ending with a wrong-side row.
Place a marker at each end of last row.
Work 10 rows more. Bind off.

right front edging

Mark a point 4 (4½: 4¾)in down from neck edge.
With wrong side facing, using a size 7 double-pointed needle, and C, pick up and k 12 (13: 14) sts along bound-off edge of neck, then with a second double-pointed needle, pick up and k 23 (25: 28) sts down front edge to marker. Break off yarn.
With right side of front facing, size 7 needle, and C, pick up and k 58 (63: 68) sts up right front to marker, break off yarn, slip 23 (25: 28) sts from second double-pointed needle onto same needle.
With wrong side of front (right side of collar) facing, return to first double-pointed needle, p35 (38: 42), k58 (63: 68).
Bind-off row Bind off 58 (63: 68) sts knitwise, then 35 (38: 42) sts purlwise.

left front edging

Mark a point 4 (4¹/₂: 4³/₄)in from neck edge.
With wrong side facing, a size 7 double-pointed needle, and C, pick up and k 23 (25: 28) sts up front edge from marker to neck edge, then with a second double-pointed needle, pick up and k 12 (13: 14) sts along bound-off edge of neck.
Break off yarn.
With right side of front facing, size 7 needle, and C, pick up and k 58 (63: 68) sts down left front.
Next row K58 (63: 68), p35 (38: 42).
Bind-off row Bind off 35 (38: 42) sts purlwise, then 58 (63: 68) sts knitwise.

to finish

Stitching row ends of sleeve above markers to sts bound off at underarm, sew sleeves into armholes, easing to fit. Sew side and sleeve seams, reversing seam on cuff. Sew row ends of front edging to collar edging. Sew on buttons.

time out

sizes and measurements

To fit ages 2–3 (3–4: 4–5) years

finished measurements

Chest 24³/₄ (26¹/₂: 28)in

Length to center back neck 11³/₄ (13: 14¹/₄)in

Sleeve length 8³/₄ (10: 11)in

materials

5 (6: 6) x 1³/₄oz/50g balls Debbie Bliss Baby Cashmerino in red (M)

1 (1: 1) x 1³/₄oz/50g ball Debbie Bliss Baby Cashmerino in gray (C)

Pair each of sizes 2 and 3 knitting needles

Size 2 circular knitting needle

4 small buttons

gauge

25 sts and 34 rows to 4in square over St st using size 3 needles.

classic cardigan

back

With size 2 needles and C, cast on 82 (86: 94) sts.
1st rib row K2, [p2, k2] to end.
2nd rib row P2, [k2, p2] to end.
Change to M.
Next row K to end.
Work 5 rows more in rib and inc 2 sts across last row on 2nd size only. 82 (88: 94) sts.
Change to size 3 needles.
Beg with a k row, work in St st until back measures 6$\frac{3}{4}$ (7$\frac{1}{2}$: 8$\frac{1}{4}$)in from cast-on edge, ending with a p row.
Shape raglan armholes
Bind off 4 sts at beg of next 2 rows. 74 (80: 86) sts.
Next row K2, skp, k to last 4 sts, k2tog, k2.
Next row P to end.
Rep the last 2 rows until 30 (32: 34) sts rem, ending with a p row. Bind off.

left front

With size 2 needles and C, cast on 39 (39: 43) sts.
1st rib row K2, [p2, k2] to last 5 sts, p2, k3.
2nd rib row P3, [k2, p2] to end.
**Change to M and k 1 row.
Work 5 rows more in rib and inc 2 sts across last row on 2nd size only. 39 (41: 43) sts.
Change to size 3 needles.
Beg with a k row, work in St st until left front measures 6$\frac{3}{4}$ (7$\frac{1}{2}$: 8$\frac{1}{4}$)in from cast-on edge, ending with a p row.**
Shape raglan armhole
Next row (right side) Bind off 4 sts, k to last 4 sts, k2tog, k2. 34 (36: 38) sts.
Next row P to end.
Next row K2, skp, k to end.
Next row P to end.
Next row K2, skp, k to last 4 sts, k2tog, k2.
Next row P to end.
Rep the last 4 rows 9 times more. 4 (6: 8) sts
Next row K2, skp, k to end.
Next row P to end. 3 (5: 7) sts.
2nd and 3rd sizes only
Rep the last 2 rows -(2: 4) times more. 3 sts.
All sizes
Next row K1, skp.
Next row P to end. Bind off.

right front

With size 2 needles and C, cast on 39 (39: 43) sts.
1st rib row K3, [p2, k2] to end.
2nd rib row P2, [k2, p2] to last 5 sts, k2, p3.
Work as Left Front from ** to **.
Shape raglan armhole
Next row (right side) K2, skp, k to end.

Next row Bind off 4 sts, p to end. 34 (36: 38) sts.
Next row K to last 4 sts, k2tog, k2.
Next row P to end.
Next row K2, skp, k to last 4 sts, k2tog, k2.
Next row P to end.
Rep the last 4 rows 9 times more. 4 (6: 8) sts
Next row K to last 4 sts, k2tog, k2.
Next row P to end. 3 (5: 7) sts.
2nd and 3rd sizes only
Rep the last 2 rows -(2: 4) times more. 3 sts.
All sizes
Next row K2tog, k1.
Next row P to end. Bind off.

sleeves

With size 2 needles and C, cast on 42 (46: 50) sts.
1st rib row K2, [p2, k2] to end.
2nd rib row P2, [k2, p2] to end.
Change to M.
Next row K to end.
Work 5 rows more in rib.
Change to size 3 needles.
Beg with a k row, work in St st.
Work 4 rows.
Inc row K3, M1, k to last 3 sts, M1, k3.
Work 5 rows.
Rep the last 6 rows until there are 62 (70: 78) sts.
Work even until sleeve measures 8³⁄₄ (10: 11)in from cast-on edge, ending with a p row.
Shape raglan sleeve top
Bind off 4 sts at beg of next 2 rows. 54 (62: 70) sts.
Next row K2, skp, k to last 4 sts, k2tog, k2.
Next row P to end.
Rep the last 2 rows until 10 (14: 18) sts rem, ending with a p row. Bind off.

front and neck band

Sew raglan seams.
With right side facing, size 2 circular needle, and C, pick up and k 43 (48: 53) up right front edge to
beg of neck shaping, 34 (36: 38) sts along right front neck edge, 8 (12: 16) sts from top of right sleeve,
28 (30: 32) sts from back neck, 8 (12: 16) sts from top of left sleeve, pick up and k 34 (36: 38) sts down
left front neck edge to beg of neck shaping, 43 (48: 53) down left front edge. 198 (222: 246) sts.
1st rib row P2, [k2, p2] to end.
2nd rib row K2, [p2, k2] to end.
Buttonhole row (wrong side) Rib 157 (175: 193), [rib 2tog, yo, rib 10 (12: 14)] 3 times, k2tog, yo, rib 3.
Rib 2 more rows. Bind off in rib.

to finish

Sew side and sleeve seams. Sew underarm seam. Sew on buttons.

sizes and measurements

To fit ages 2–3 (3–4: 4–5) years

finished measurements

Chest 24 (26: 28)in

Length to shoulder 11³/₄ (13: 14¹/₄)in

materials

4 (4: 5) x 1³/₄oz/50g balls Debbie Bliss Baby Cashmerino in gray (M)

1 (1: 1) x 1³/₄oz/50g ball Debbie Bliss Baby Cashmerino in red (C)

Pair each of sizes 2 and 3 knitting needles

gauge

25 sts and 34 rows to 4in square over St st using size 3 needles.

abbreviations

See page 23.

112

v−neck vest

back

With size 2 needles and C, cast on 78 (82: 90) sts.

1st rib row K2, [p2, k2] to end.

2nd rib row P2, [k2, p2] to end.

Change to M.

Next row K to end.

Work 5 rows more in rib and inc 2 sts evenly across last row on 2nd size only. 78 (84: 90) sts.

Change to size 3 needles.

Beg with a k row, work in St st until back measures 6³/₄ (7¹/₂: 8¹/₄)in from cast-on edge, ending with a p row.

Shape armholes

Bind off 6 sts at beg of next 2 rows. 66 (72: 78) sts.**

Next row K2, skp, k to last 2 sts, k2tog, k2.

Next row P to end.

Rep the last 2 rows 5 times more. 54 (60: 66) sts.

Cont in St st until back measures 11³/₄ (13: 14¹/₄)in from cast-on edge, ending with a p row.

Shape shoulders

Bind off 15 (16: 17) sts at beg of next 2 rows.

Leave rem 24 (28: 32) sts on a spare needle.

front	Work as given for Back to **.
	Shape neck
	Next row (right side) K2, skp, k24 (27: 30), k2tog, k2, turn and work on these sts for first side of neck.
	Next row P to end.
	Next row K2, skp, k to last 4 sts, k2tog, k2.
	Rep the last 2 rows 4 times more. 20 (23: 26) sts.
	Keeping armhole edge straight, cont to dec at neck edge on every foll 4th row until 15 (16: 17) sts rem.
	Work even until front measures same as Back to shoulder, ending with a p row.
	Bind off.
	With right side facing, slip center 2 sts onto a safety pin, and join on yarn to rem sts.
	Next row K2, skp, k24 (27: 30), k2tog, k2.
	Next row P to end.
	Next row K2, skp, k to last 4 sts, k2tog, k2.
	Rep the last 2 rows 4 times more. 20 (23: 26) sts.
	Keeping armhole edge straight, cont to dec at neck edge on every foll 4th row until 15 (16: 17) sts rem.
	Work even until front measures same as Back to shoulder, ending with a p row.
	Bind off.

neckband	Sew right shoulder seam.
	With right side facing, size 2 needles, and M, pick up and k 34 (38: 42) sts evenly down left side of front neck, k2 from safety pin, pick up and k 34 (38: 42) sts evenly up right side of front neck, k 24 (28: 32) sts from back neck holder. 94 (106: 118) sts.
	1st row K2, [p2, k2] to end.
	2nd row Rib 33 (37: 41), k2tog, skp, rib to end.
	3rd row Rib to end.
	4th row Rib 32 (36: 40), k2tog, skp, rib to end.
	5th row Rib to end.
	Change to C.
	6th row K31 (35: 39), k2tog, skp, k to end.
	7th row Rib to end.
	Bind off in rib, and dec on this row as before.

armbands	Sew left shoulder and neckband seam.
	With right side facing, size 2 needles, and M, pick up and k 86 (94: 102) sts along armhole edge.
	Work 5 rows in rib as given for Back.
	Change to C.
	6th row K to end.
	7th row Rib to end.
	Bind off in rib.

to finish	Sew side and armband seams.

sizes and measurements

To fit ages 2–3 (3–4: 4–5) years

finished measurements

Chest 30³/₄ (32¹/₄: 33³/₄)in
Length to shoulder 19³/₄ (21¹/₄: 22³/₄)in
Sleeve length, with cuff turned back 9¹/₂ (10³/₄: 11³/₄)in

materials

15 (16: 17) x 1³/₄oz/50g balls Debbie Bliss Rialto Aran in pale blue
Pair each of sizes 7 and 8 knitting needles
16 (18: 20)in open-ended zipper

gauge

19 sts and 36 rows to 4in square over seed st using size 8 needles.

abbreviations

yo2 = yarn around right-hand needle twice to make 2 new sts.
Also see page 23.

anorak

back

Right side
With size 7 needles, cast on 40 (42: 44) sts.
K 3 rows.
Change to size 8 needles.
Next row [P1, k1] to last 4 sts, k4.
Next row (wrong side) K4, [k1, p1] 2 (3: 4) times, turn.
Next row [P1, k1] 2 (3: 4) times, k4.
Next row K4, [k1, p1] 4 (5: 6) times, turn.
Next row [P1, k1] 4 (5: 6) times, k4.
Next row K4, [k1, p1] 6 (7: 8) times, turn.
Next row [P1, k1] 6 (7: 8) times, k4.
Next row K4, [k1, p1] 8 (9: 10) times, turn.
Next row [P1, k1] 8 (9: 10) times, k4.
Cont in this way, working an extra 4 sts on every alt row until all the sts have been taken into
seed st with 5 sts in garter st, ending with a right-side row.
Place a marker at beg of last row.
Next row (wrong side) K5, seed st to end.
Next row Seed st to last 5 sts, k5.
Rep the last 2 rows until side seam (seed-st edge) measures 9 (10¹/₄: 11¹/₂)in from cast-on edge,
ending with a right-side row.

Break off yarn and leave these sts on a holder.

Mark the position on the garter-st edging for 4 buttons, the first level with marker, the fourth 1$\frac{1}{2}$in below top edge with two spaced evenly between.

Left side

With size 7 needles, cast on 40 (42: 44) sts.

K 3 rows.

Change to size 8 needles.

Next row (right side) K4, [k1, p1] 2 (3: 4) times, turn.

Next row [P1, k1] 2 (3: 4) times, k4.

Next row K4, [k1, p1] 4 (5: 6) times, turn,

Next row [P1, k1] 4 (5: 6) times, k4.

Next row K4, [k1, p1] 6 (7: 8) times, turn.

Next row [P1, k1] 6 (7: 8) times, k4.

Next row K4, [k1, p1] 8 (9: 10) times, turn.

Next row [P1, k1] 8 (9: 10) times, k4.

Cont in this way, working an extra 4 sts on every alt row until all the sts have been taken into seed st with 5 sts in garter st, ending with a wrong-side row.

Buttonhole row K1, k2tog, yo2, skp, seed st to end.

Cont in seed st and garter-st patt, working buttonholes to match markers, until side seam (seed-st edge) measures 9 (10$\frac{1}{4}$: 11$\frac{1}{2}$)in from cast-on edge, ending with a right-side row.

Joining row (wrong side) Seed st 35 (37: 39), place right back on top of left back, [k next st of left back tog with next st of right back] 5 times, seed st to end. 75 (79: 83) sts

Cord channel

Beg with a k row, work 4 rows in St st.

Do not break off yarn and leave these sts on a spare needle.

Channel back

With wrong side facing, working down through sts, miss first st, then pick up and k 1 st from each st along first k row, miss last st, turn. (This will be wrong side of work facing but "right" side of St st.)

Beg with a k row, work 4 rows St st.

Break off yarn and slip stitches from one needle to another.

Return to main part.

Next row K1, [k next st of main part tog with next st of channel back] 73 (77: 81) times, k1. 75 (79: 83) sts.

Cont in seed st until back measures 14$\frac{3}{4}$ (15$\frac{3}{4}$: 17)in from cast-on edge, ending with a wrong-side row.

Shape armholes

Bind off 6 sts at beg of next 2 rows. 63 (67: 71) sts.

Work even until back measures 19$\frac{3}{4}$ (21$\frac{1}{4}$: 22$\frac{3}{4}$)in from cast-on edge, ending with a wrong-side row.

Shape shoulders

Bind off 10 (10: 11) sts at beg of next 2 rows and 10 (11: 11) sts at beg of foll 2 rows.

Bind off rem 23 (25: 27) sts.

left front

With size 7 needles, cast on 38 (40: 42) sts.

K 3 rows.

Change to size 8 needles.

1st row (right side) [K1, p1] to last 2 sts, k2.

2nd row K2, [p1, k1] to end.

These 2 rows form seed st with garter-st front edging.

Cont in seed st until front measures 9 (10¼: 11½)in from cast-on edge, ending with a wrong-side row.

Cord channel

Next row K28 (30: 32), turn and leave rem 10 sts on a spare needle.

Next row K2, p to end.

Next row K to end.

Next row K2, p to end.

Do not break off yarn and leave these sts on a holder.

With wrong side facing, working down through sts, miss first st, then pick up and k 1 st from each st along first k row, 22 (29: 31) times, then patt across 10 sts on holder. (This will be wrong side of work facing but "right" side of St st.)

Next row Patt 10 sts, k to end.

Next row P to last 10 sts, patt to end.

Next row Patt 10 sts, k to end.

Break off yarn.

Return to main part.

Next row K1, [k next st of main part tog with next st of channel back] 22 (29: 31) times, patt to end. 38 (40: 42) sts.

Cont in seed st with garter-st edging until front measures 14¾ (15¾: 17)in from cast-on edge, ending with a wrong-side row.

Shape armhole

Bind off 6 sts at beg of next row. 32 (34: 36) sts.

Work even until front measures 17¾ (19¼: 21)in from cast-on edge, ending with a wrong-side row.

Shape neck

Next row Patt to last 6 (7: 8) sts, turn and work on these 26 (27: 28) sts only, leave rem 6 (7: 8) sts on a holder for hood.

Dec 1 st at neck edge on next 6 rows. 20 (21: 22) sts.

Work even until front matches Back to shoulder, ending at side edge.

Shape shoulder

Bind off 10 (10: 11) sts at beg of next row.

Work 1 row. Bind off rem 10 (11: 11) sts.

right front

With size 7 needles, cast on 38 (40: 42) sts.

K 3 rows.

Change to size 8 needles.

1st row (right side) K2, [p1, k1] to end.

2nd row [K1, p1] to last 2 sts, k2.

These 2 rows form seed st with garter-st front edging.

Cont in seed st until front measures 9 (10¼: 11½)in from cast-on edge, ending with a wrong-side row.

Cord Channel

Next row Patt 10, leave these sts on a holder, k28 (30: 32).

Next row P to last 2 sts, k2.

Next row K to end.

Next row P to last 2 sts, k2.

Break off yarn and leave these sts on a spare needle.

Slip the 10 sts from holder onto a size 8 needle, then with wrong side facing, working down through sts, pick up and k 1 st from each st along first k row, 22 (29: 31) times, k last st. (This will be wrong side of work facing but "right" side of St st.)

Next row K to last 10 sts, patt to end.

Next row Patt 10 sts, p to end.

Next row K to last 10 sts, patt to end.

Return to main part.

Next row Patt 10, [k next st of main part tog with next st of back] 22 (29: 31) times, k1. 38 (40: 42) sts.

Cont in seed st with garter-st edging until front measures 14³/₄ (15³/₄: 17)in from cast-on edge, ending with a right-side row.

Shape armhole

Bind off 6 sts at beg of next row. 32 (34: 36) sts.

Work even until front measures 17³/₄ (19¹/₄: 21)in from cast-on edge, ending with a wrong-side row.

Shape neck

Next row P6 (7: 8) sts and slip these sts onto a holder, patt to end. 26 (27: 28) sts.

Dec 1 st at neck edge on next 6 rows. 20 (21: 22) sts.

Work even until front matches Back to shoulder, ending at side edge.

Shape shoulder

Bind off 10 (10: 11) sts at beg of next row.

Work 1 row. Bind off rem 10 (11: 11) sts.

sleeves

With size 7 needles, cast on 31 (33: 35) sts.

Change to size 8 needles.

Seed st row (wrong side) P1, [k1, p1] to end.

This row forms the seed st and is repeated.

Work 12 (14: 16) rows more in seed st.

Inc and work into seed st one st at each end of the next row and every foll 8th row until there
are 47 (51: 57) sts.
Work even until sleeve measures 10³/₄ (12: 13)in from cast-on edge, ending with a wrong-side row.
Place markers at each end of last row.
Work 10 rows more.
Bind off.

hood

Sew shoulder seams.
With wrong side facing and size 7 needles, slip 6 (7: 8) sts from right front holder, onto a needle,
pick up and k 12 sts up right side of front neck, cast on 35 (39: 43) sts, pick up and k 12 sts down
left side of front neck, then patt across 6 (7: 8) sts on left front holder. 71 (77: 83) sts.
Cont in seed st with garter-st edging.
Work 3 rows.
Next row K2, M1, seed st to last 2 sts, M1, k2.
Work 7 rows.
Rep the last 8 rows 7 (8: 9) times more and the inc row again. 89 (97: 105) sts.
Work 1 row.
Next row Patt 43 (47: 51), work 3 tog, patt to end.
Next row Patt to end.
Next row Patt 42 (46: 50), work 3 tog, patt to end.
Next row Patt to end.
Next row Patt 41 (45: 49), work 3 tog, patt to end.
Next row Patt to end.
Next row Patt 40 (44: 48), work 3 tog, patt to end.
Next row Patt to end.
Bind off.

left lower pocket

**With size 8 needles, cast on 19 (21: 23) sts.
Seed st row K1, [p1, k1] to end.
This row forms seed st and is repeated.**
Cont in seed st until pocket measures 3¼ (3½: 4)in from cast-on edge, ending with a right-side row.
Shape top of pocket
Next 2 rows Seed st to last 4 sts, turn, seed st to end.
Next 2 rows Seed st to last 8 sts, turn, seed st to end.
Next 2 rows Seed st to last 12 sts, turn, seed st to end.
Next 2 rows Seed st to last 16 sts, turn, seed st to end.
Next row Seed st to end.
Change to size 7 needles.
K 2 rows.
Buttonhole row K8 (9: 10), k2tog, yo2, skp, k to end.
K 2 rows. Bind off.

right lower pocket

Work as Left Lower Pocket from ** to **.
Cont in seed st until pocket measures 3¼ (3½: 4)in from cast-on edge, ending with a wrong-side row.
Shape top of pocket
Next 2 rows Seed st to last 4 sts, turn, seed st to end.
Next 2 rows Seed st to last 8 sts, turn, seed st to end.
Next 2 rows Seed st to last 12 sts, turn, seed st to end.
Next 2 rows Seed st to last 16 sts, turn, seed st to end.
Change to size 7 needles.
K 2 rows.
Buttonhole row K7 (8: 9), k2tog, yo2, skp, k to end.
K 2 rows. Bind off.

mock pocket flap (make 2)

With size 8 needles, cast on 19 (21: 23) sts.
Patt row K2, [p1, k1] to last 3 sts, p1, k2.
Rep this row 11 times more.
K 2 rows.
Buttonhole row K8 (9: 10), k2tog, yo2, skp, k to end.
K 2 rows. Bind off.

cord

With size 7 needles, cast on 4 sts.
Beg with a k row, work in St st until tie measures 60in, ending with a p row.
Next row [K2tog] twice.
Thread yarn through remaining 2 sts and fasten off.

to finish

Sew sleeves into armholes, stitching row ends above markers to sts bound off at underarm. Sew side and sleeve seams, reversing seam on last 1¼in for turn back. Sew cast-on edge of hood to sts bound off at back neck, easing to fit. Sew on pockets and mock pocket flaps. Sew on buttons. Thread cord through channel to tie at center front. Hand sew zipper in place, beginning at neck edge.

hoodie

sizes and measurements
To fit ages 2–3 (3–4: 4–5) years
finished measurements
Chest 28³/₄ (31¹/₂: 34³/₄)in
Length to shoulder 13³/₄ (15³/₄: 17³/₄)in
Sleeve length with cuff turned back 8³/₄ (10: 11)in

materials
8 (9: 10) x 1³/₄oz/50g balls Debbie Bliss Rialto Aran in green
Pair each of sizes 7 and 8 knitting needles
Cable needle

gauge
18 sts and 24 rows to 4in square over St st using size 8 needles.

abbreviations
C4B = slip next 2 sts onto a cable needle and hold at back of work, k2, then k2 from cable needle.
C4F = slip next 2 sts onto a cable needle and hold at front of work, k2, then k2 from cable needle.
M1pw = make 1 st by picking up and purling into back of loop lying between st just worked and next st.
Also see page 23.

back

With size 7 needles, cast on 66 (74: 82) sts.
1st row K2, [p2, k2] to end.
2nd row P2, [k2, p2] to end.
Rep the last 2 rows 5 times more, inc 2 sts across last row on 1st size only. 68 (74: 82) sts.
Change to size 8 needles.
Beg with a k row, work in St st until back measures 8¼ (9¾: 11½)in from cast-on edge, ending with a p row.
Shape armholes
Next row Bind off 7 (6: 5) sts, k to end.
Next row Bind off 7 (6: 5) sts, with 1 st on needle after bind-off, p next 5 (9: 9) sts, [M1pw, p2, M1pw, p8] 4 (4: 5) times, M1pw, p2, M1pw, p6 (10: 10). 64 (72: 84) sts.
Work in yoke patt as follows:
1st row (right side) P1, [k2, p2] 1 (2: 2) times, [k2, C4F, p2, k2, p2] 4 (4: 5) times, k2, C4F, [p2, k2] 1 (2: 2) times, p1.
2nd row K1, [p2, k2] 1 (2: 2) times, p6, [k2, p2, k2, p6] 4 (4: 5) times, [k2, p2] 1 (2: 2) times, k1.
3rd row P1, [k2, p2] 1 (2: 2) times, [C4B, k2, p2, k2, p2] 4 (4: 5) times, C4B, k2, [p2, k2] 1 (2: 2) times, p1.
4th row K1, [p2, k2] 1 (2: 2) times, p6, [k2, p2, k2, p6] 4 (4: 5) times, [k2, p2] 1 (2: 2) times, k1.
These 4 rows form the patt and are repeated.**
Cont in patt until back measures 13 (15: 17)in from cast-on edge, ending with a wrong-side row.
Shape back neck
Next row Patt 21 (24: 29), turn and work on these sts only for first side of neck shaping.
Next row Patt 2 tog, patt to end.
Next row Patt to last 2 sts, patt 2 tog.
Next row Patt to end. 19 (22: 27) sts.
Bind off.
With right side facing, slip center 22 (24: 26) sts onto a holder, rejoin yarn to rem sts, patt to end.
Complete to match first side, reversing shaping.

front

Work as given for Back to **.
Cont in patt until front measures 11¾ (13½: 15)in from cast-on edge, ending with a wrong-side row.
Shape front neck
Next row Patt 24 (27: 32), turn and work on these sts for first side of neck shaping.
Dec 1 st at neck on every foll alt row until 19 (22: 27) sts rem.
Work even until front measures same as Back to shoulder, ending at armhole edge.
Bind off.
With right side facing, slip center 16 (18: 20) sts onto a holder, rejoin yarn to rem sts, patt to end.
Complete to match first side, reversing shaping.

sleeves

With size 7 needles, cast on 34 (38: 42) sts.
1st row K2, [p2, k2] to end.
2nd row P2, [k2, p2] to end.
Rep the last 2 rows 5 times more.
Change to size 8 needles
Beg with a k row, work in St st.

Work 2 rows.
Inc row K3, M1, k to last 3 sts, M1, k3.
Work 3 rows.
Rep the last 4 rows 7 (8: 9) times more and the inc row again. 52 (58: 64) sts.
Next row P5 (8: 6) sts, [M1pw, p2, M1pw, p8] 4 (4: 5) times, M1pw, p2, M1pw, p5 (8: 6). 62 (68: 76) sts.
Cont in patt as follows:
1st row K2 (5: 3), p2, [k2, C4F, p2, k2, p2] 4 (4: 5) times, k2, C4F, p2, k2 (5: 3).
2nd row P2 (5: 3), k2, p6, [k2, p2, k2, p6] 4 (4: 5) times, k2, p2 (5: 3).
3rd row K2 (5: 3), p2, [C4B, k2, p2, k2, p2] 4 (4: 5) times, C4B, k2, p2, k2 (5: 3).
4th row P2 (5: 3), k2, p6, [k2, p2, k2, p6] 4 (4: 5) times, k2, p2 (5: 3).
These 4 rows form the patt and are repeated.
Cont in patt until sleeve measures 8³/₄ (10: 11)in from cast-on edge, ending with a wrong-side row.
Place markers at each end of last row.
Work 10 rows more. Bind off.

neckband

Sew right shoulder seam.
With right side facing and size 7 needles, pick up and k 11 sts down left front neck, k across 16 (18: 20) sts from front neck, pick up and k 11 sts up right front neck, 5 sts down right back neck, k across 22 (24: 26) sts from back neck, then pick up and k 5 sts up left back neck. 70 (74: 78) sts.
1st row P2, [k2, p2] to end.
2nd row K2, [p2, k2] to end.
Rep the last 2 rows once more and the 1st row again.
Bind off in rib.

hood

With size 8 needles, cast on 86 (94: 102) sts.
Beg with a k row, work in St st until hood measures 8 (9: 10¼)in from cast-on edge, ending with a p row.
Change to size 7 needles.
1st row K2, [p2, k2] to end.
2nd row P2, [k2, p2] to end.
Rep the last 2 rows twice more.
Bind off in rib.

pocket

With size 7 needles, cast on 24 (28: 30) sts.
1st row K3, [p2, k2] to last 5 sts, p2, k3.
2nd row P3, [k2, p2] to last 5 sts, k2, p3.
Rep the last 2 rows twice more.
Change to size 8 needles.
Beg with a k row, work in St st until pocket measures 6¼ (7: 8)in, ending with a p row.
Change to size 7 needles.
1st row K3, [p2, k2] to last 5 sts, p2, k3.
2nd row P3, [k2, p2] to last 5 sts, k2, p3.
Rep the last 2 rows twice more.
Bind off.

to finish

Sew left shoulder and neckband seam. Sew sleeves into armholes, stitching row ends above markers to sts bound off at underarm. Sew side and sleeve seams. Sew pocket to front. Fold hood in half and sew together cast-on edges to form back seam. Sew hood in place inside neckband.

measurements
Length approximately 8$\frac{1}{4}$in
Height approximately 3$\frac{1}{2}$in

materials
1 x 1$\frac{3}{4}$oz/50g ball of Debbie Bliss Rialto DK in each of red (A), pink (B), lime (C), gray (D), and duck egg (E) OR approximately 20yd in each of 5 shades of Debbie Bliss Rialto DK
Pair of size 5 knitting needles
8in x 9$\frac{1}{4}$in piece of lining fabric
8in zipper
Sewing thread and sewing needle

gauge
24 sts and 48 rows to 4in square over garter st using size 5 needles.

abbreviations
See page 23.

pencil case

to make

With size 5 needles and A, cast on 42 sts.
K 1 row.
Cont in garter st (k every row), change color and work 2-row stripes of each color randomly until work measures 8$\frac{1}{4}$in, ending with the 1st row of a 2-row stripe in A.
Bind off knitwise in A.

to finish

Fold knitting in half lengthwise and sew together folded cast-on and bound-off edges, so leaving row-end edges open. Pin, baste, and hand stitch zipper in place, tucking all yarn ends in behind zipper tape and taking care to match stripes.
Fold lining fabric in half lengthwise and taking $\frac{1}{2}$in seams, sew together folded short ends.
Press $\frac{1}{2}$in around open edges onto wrong side. Insert lining into pencil case and hand stitch lining to zipper tape.
Cut a few lengths of assorted yarn colors and thread through zipper pull to assist opening and closing of pencil case.

measurements
Approximately 8in x 9^1/$_2$in x 2in

materials
5 x 1^3/$_4$oz/50g balls Debbie Bliss Rialto DK in navy (M)
1 x 1^3/$_4$oz/50g ball Debbie Bliss Rialto DK in red (C)
Pair of size 7 knitting needles
^{5}/$_8$yd of lining fabric
42in of 1^1/$_2$in wide red cotton tape
2 kilt straps with buckles

gauge
18^1/$_2$ sts and 27 rows to 4in square over St st using size 7 needles and two strands of
yarn held together.

notes
The satchel is worked in one piece starting at the lower edge of the front flap.
Two strands of yarn held together are used throughout.

satchel

to make

Front flap
With size 7 needles and two strands of M held together throughout, cast on 41 sts.
Seed st row K1, [p1, k1] to end.
Rep this row 3 times more.
Next row (right side) [K1, p1] twice, k33, [p1, k1] twice.
Next row [K1, p1] twice, p33, [p1, k1] twice.
Rep the last 2 rows until work measures 4^3/$_4$in from cast-on edge, ending with a wrong-side row.
Seed st 4 rows.
Next row [K1, p1] twice, k33, [p1, k1] twice.
Ridge row [K1, p1] twice, k33, [p1, k1] twice.
Back
Next row [K1, p1] twice, k33, [p1, k1] twice.
Seed st 4 rows.
**Next row (wrong side) [K1, p1] twice, p33, [p1, k1] twice.
Next row [K1, p1] twice, k33, [p1, k1] twice.
Rep the last 2 rows for 6^1/$_4$in from **, ending with a wrong-side row.
Seed st 4 rows.
Next row [K1, p1] twice, k33, [p1, k1] twice.
Ridge row (wrong side) [K1, p1] twice, k33, [p1, k1] twice.

Base
Next row [K1, p1] twice, k33, [p1, k1] twice.
Seed st 4 rows.
Next row (wrong side) [K1, p1] twice, p33, [p1, k1] twice.
Next row [K1, p1] twice, k33, [p1, k1] twice.
Rep the last 2 rows once more and the first of these 2 rows again.
Seed st 4 rows.
Next row [K1, p1] twice, k33, [p1, k1] twice.
Ridge row (wrong side) [K1, p1] twice, k33, [p1, k1] twice.
Front
Next row [K1, p1] twice, k33, [p1, k1] twice.
Seed st 4 rows.
Next row (wrong side) [K1, p1] twice, p33, [p1, k1] twice.
Next row [K1, p1] twice, k33, [p1, k1] twice.
Rep the last 2 rows 4 times more and the first of these 2 rows again.
Next row (right side) With M, [k1, p1] twice, k6, with C, k21, with M, k6, [p1, k1] twice.
Next row With M, [k1, p1] twice, p6, with C, p21, with M, p6, [p1, k1] twice.
Rep the last 2 rows 10 times more.
Next row With M, [k1, p1] twice, p33, [p1, k1] twice.
Cont in M only and work 4 rows in seed st.
Bind off in seed st.

gusset strap

With size 7 needles and two strands of M held together throughout, cast on 9 sts.
Seed st row K1, [p1, k1] to end.
Rep this row until gusset strap measures approximately 39¹/₂in from cast-on edge.
Bind off in seed st.

front pocket

With size 7 needles and two strands of M held together throughout, cast on 29 sts.
Seed st row K1, [p1, k1] to end.
Rep the last row 3 times more.
1st row [K1, p1] twice, k21, [p1, k1] twice.
2nd row {K1, p1] twice, p21, [p1, k1] to end.
Rep these 2 rows 8 times more.
Shape gusset
Next 2 rows Bind off 4 sts, seed st to end. 21 sts.
Work 5 rows in seed st for pocket base.
Bind off in seed st.

to finish

Sew short bound-off edges of pocket to seed-st row ends of pocket base. Sew side and base edges of pocket to contrasting color area on satchel front. Sew red tape to gusset strip to prevent over-stretching. Sew cast-on and bound-off edges of gusset strip to row ends of satchel base between ridge rows. Sew edges of satchel front to gusset strip. Sew edges of satchel back to gusset strip from base to end of St st section. Hand stitch kilt straps to front of satchel, each side of pocket.

lining

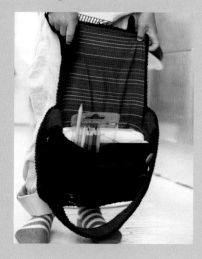

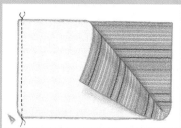

fig 1

fig 2

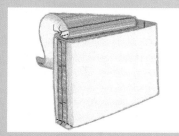

fig 3

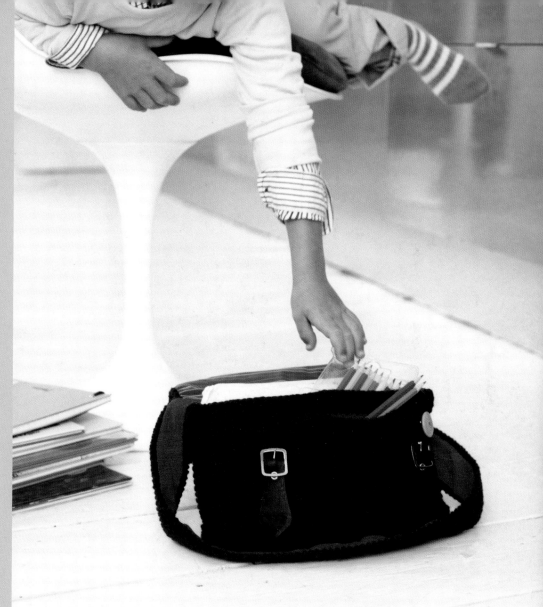

For the main bag, cut a piece of lining fabric $12\frac{1}{4}$in x 14in. Fold in half to make a rectangle $12\frac{1}{4}$in x 7in and sew the side seams, taking a $\frac{5}{8}$in seam allowance. Clip corners at the fold and press seams open. Refold and stitch 2in across the points to form the base, and trim away excess fabric.

For the satchel flap lining, cut a second piece of fabric $8\frac{1}{2}$in x 10in. With right sides together and taking a $\frac{5}{8}$in seam allowance, stitch one longer side centrally to the top edge of the main bag lining, leaving $\frac{5}{8}$in at each end of seam unstitched. Press seam open and continue to press $\frac{5}{8}$in around top of main bag lining onto wrong side, then press $\frac{5}{8}$in around the three unstitched edges of flap lining onto wrong side. Insert lining into satchel and slipstitch in place around pressed edges.

scarf coat

sizes and measurements
To fit ages 2–3 (3–4: 4–5) years
finished measurements
Chest 30 (31$\frac{1}{2}$: 33$\frac{1}{2}$)in
Length to shoulder 19 (20$\frac{1}{2}$: 22)in
Sleeve length, with cuff turned back 9$\frac{1}{2}$ (10$\frac{1}{2}$: 11$\frac{3}{4}$)in

materials
10 (12: 14) x 1$\frac{3}{4}$oz/50g balls Debbie Bliss Rialto Aran in berry (M)
1 (1: 1) x 1$\frac{3}{4}$oz/50g ball Debbie Bliss Rialto Aran in pale blue (C)
Pair each of sizes 7 and 8 knitting needles
Size 8 circular knitting needle
2 large buttons

gauge
18 sts and 30 rows to 4in square over seed st using size 8 needles.

abbreviations
yo2 = yarn around right-hand needle twice to make 2 new sts.
Also see page 23.

back

With size 7 needles and M, cast on 89 (93: 97) sts.
K 3 rows.
Change to size 8 needles.
Seed st row K1, [p1, k1] to end.
Repeating last row to form seed st, work 9 (15: 21) rows more in seed st.
Dec row (right side) Seed st 6, k3tog, seed st to last 9 sts, k3tog, seed st 6.
Seed st 19 rows.
Rep the last 20 rows 3 times more and the dec row again. 69 (73: 77) sts.
Seed st 7 rows.
Shape armholes
Bind off 4 sts at beg of next 2 rows. 61 (65: 69) sts.
Leave these sts on a spare needle.

left front

With size 7 needles and M, cast on 47 (49: 51) sts.
K 3 rows.
Change to size 8 needles.
Next row P1, [k1, p1] to last 6 sts, k6.
Next row K6, p1, [k1, p1] to end.
These 2 rows form the seed st with garter-st edging.
Work 8 (14: 20) rows more.

Dec row (right side) Seed st 6, p3tog, seed st to last to last 6 sts, k6.
Patt 19 rows.
Dec row (right side) Seed st 6, p3tog, seed st to last to last 6 sts, k6. 43 (45: 47) sts.
Patt 3 rows.

Pocket opening
Next row Seed st 16 (18: 20), turn and work on these sts only, leave rem 27 sts on a holder.
Work 15 rows.
Dec row (right side) Seed st 6, p3tog, seed st to end.
Work 14 rows.
Leave these sts on a holder.
With right side facing, rejoin yarn to rem sts, patt to end.
Work 30 rows more, so ending with a right-side row.
Next row Seed st 27, then with wrong side of first side facing, seed st to end. 41 (43: 45) sts.
Work 4 rows.
Dec row (right side) Seed st 6, p3tog, seed st to last to last 6 sts, k6.
Patt 19 rows.
Dec row (right side) Seed st 6, p3tog, seed st to last to last 6 sts, k6. 37 (39: 41) sts.
Patt 7 rows.

Shape armholes
Bind off 4 sts at beg of next row. 33 (35: 37) sts.
Patt 1 row.
Leave these sts on a spare needle.

right front

With size 7 needles and M, cast on 47 (49: 51) sts.
K 3 rows.
Change to size 8 needles.
Next row K6, p1, [k1, p1] to end.
Next row P1, [k1, p1] to last 6 sts, k6.
These 2 rows form the seed st with garter-st edging.
Work 8 (14: 20) rows more.
Dec row (right side) K6, seed st to last 9 sts, p3tog, seed st 6.
Patt 19 rows.
Dec row K6, seed st to last 9 sts, p3tog, seed st 6. 43 (45: 47) sts.
Patt 3 rows.

Pocket opening
Next row (right side) K6, seed st 21, turn and work on these sts only, leave rem 16 (18: 20) sts on a holder.
Work 30 rows, so ending with a right-side row.
Leave these sts on a holder.
With right side facing, rejoin yarn to rem 16 (18: 20) sts, patt to end.
Work 15 rows.
Dec row Seed st to last 9 sts, p3tog, seed st 6.
Work 14 rows.
Next row Seed st 14 (16: 18) then with wrong side of first side facing, seed st to end. 41 (43: 47) sts.
Work 4 rows.

Dec row K6, seed st to last 9 sts, p3tog, seed st 6.
Patt 19 rows.
Dec row K6, seed st to last 9 sts, p3tog, seed st 6. 37 (39: 41) sts.
Patt 8 rows.
Shape armhole
Bind off 4 sts at beg of next row. 33 (35: 37) sts.
Leave these sts on a spare needle.

left sleeve

With size 7 needles and M, cast on 30 (34: 38) sts.
K 3 rows.
Change to size 8 needles.
1st seed st row (right side of cuff, wrong side of sleeve) [P1, k1] to end.
2nd seed st row [K1, p1] to end.
Work 11 (13: 15) rows more in seed st.
Place markers at each end of last row.
Change to size 7 needles.
Work 12 (14:16) rows.
Change to size 8 needles.
Inc and work into seed st one st at each end of 3rd (5th: 7th) row and every foll 6th row until there
are 50 (54: 58) sts.
Work even until sleeve measures 9$\frac{1}{2}$ (10$\frac{1}{2}$: 11$\frac{3}{4}$)in from markers, ending with a wrong-side row.
Shape top of sleeve
Bind off 4 sts at beg of next 2 rows. 42 (46: 50) sts.
Leave these sts on a spare needle.

right sleeve

Work as given for Left Sleeve, reading k for p and p for k.

yoke

With right side facing and size 8 circular needle, k6, seed st 26 (28: 30) across sts of right front,
work last st tog with first st of right sleeve, seed st 40 (44: 48), work last st of sleeve tog with first st
of back, seed st 59 (63: 67), work last st of back tog with first st of left sleeve, seed st 40 (44: 48),
work last st of sleeve tog with first st of left front, seed st 26 (28: 30), k7. 207 (223: 239) sts.
Patt row K6, seed st to last 6 sts, k6.
Patt 2 rows.
4th row Patt 31 (33: 35), work 3 tog, seed st 38 (42: 46), work 3 tog, seed st 57 (61: 65), work 3 tog,
seed st 38 (42: 46), work 3 tog, patt 31 (33: 35). 199 (215: 231) sts.
Patt 3 rows.
8th row Patt 30 (32: 34), work 3 tog, seed st 36 (40: 44), work 3 tog, seed st 55 (59: 63), work 3 tog,
seed st 36 (40: 44), work 3 tog, patt 30 (32: 34). 191 (207: 223) sts.
Patt 3 rows.
12th row Patt 29 (31: 33), work 3 tog, seed st 34 (38: 42), work 3 tog, seed st 53 (57: 61), work 3 tog,
seed st 34 (38: 42), work 3 tog, patt 29 (31: 33). 183 (199: 215) sts.
Patt 1 row.
Buttonhole row K2, k2tog, yo2, skp, patt to end.
Patt 1 row.

Working a buttonhole on the foll 25th (27th: 29th) row, cont in this way to dec 8 sts on next row and 3 foll 4th rows, then on 11 (12: 13) foll right-side rows. 63 (71: 79) sts.
Next row (wrong side) Bind off 17 (19: 21) sts, cast on 41 (43: 45), seed st to end, cast on 51 sts. 138 (146: 154) sts.
Work 1¼in in seed st, ending with a wrong-side row.
Next row Seed st 31, bind off 14 sts, seed st to end.
Next row Seed st to end, casting on 14 sts over those bound off in previous row.
Seed st 3¼in more.
Bind off in seed st.

right pocket lining

With right side facing, size 7 needles, and C, pick up and k 20 sts along back edge of pocket opening.
Next row P to end.
Next row Cast on 9 (11: 13) sts, k to end.
Work 21 (23: 25) rows more in St st.
Bind off.

left pocket lining

With right side facing, size 7 needles, and C, pick up and k 20 sts along back edge of pocket opening.
Next row P to end.
Next row K to end.
Next row Cast on 9 (11: 13) sts, p to end.
Work 21 (23: 25) rows more in St st. Bind off.

to finish

Sew side and sleeve seams, reversing seam below markers. Sew underarm seam. Sew on buttons. Slipstitch pocket linings in place.

yarn distributors

For stockists of Debbie Bliss
yarns please contact:

USA
Knitting Fever Inc.
315 Bayview Avenue
Amityville
NY 11701
USA
t: +1 516 546 3600
f: +1 516 546 6871
w: www.knittingfever.com

UK & WORLDWIDE DISTRIBUTORS
Designer Yarns Ltd.
Units 8–10
Newbridge Industrial Estate
Pitt Street, Keighley
W. Yorkshire BD21 4PQ
UK
t: +44 (0) 1535 664222
f: +44 (0) 1535 664333
e: alex@designeryarns.uk.com
w: www.designeryarns.uk.com

CANADA
Diamond Yarns Ltd
155 Martin Ross Avenue Unit 3
Toronto
Ontario M3J 2L9
Canada
t: +1 416 736 6111
f: +1 416 736 6112
w: www.diamondyarn.com

BELGIUM/HOLLAND
Pavan
Meerlaanstraat 73
9860 Balegem (Oostrezele)
Belgium
t: +32 (0) 9 221 85 94
f: +32 (0) 9 221 56 62
e: pavan@pandora.be

DENMARK
Fancy Knit
Hovedvejen 71
8586 Oerum Djurs
Ramten
Denmark
t: +45 59 46 21 89
f: +45 59 46 8018
e: roenneburg@mail.dk

FINLAND
Duo Design
Kaikukuja 1 c 31
00530 Helsinki
Finland
t: +358 (0) 9 753 1716
e: maria.hellbom@priima.net
w: www.duodesign.fi

FRANCE
Elle Tricote
8 Rue du Coq
La Petite France
67000 Strasbourg
France
t: +33 (0) 388 230313
f: +33 (0) 8823 0169
w: www.elletricote.com

GERMANY/AUSTRIA/
SWITZERLAND/LUXEMBOURG
Designer Yarns (Deutschland)
GmbH
Sachsstraße 30
D-50259 Pulheim-Brauweiler
Germany
t: +49 (0) 2234 205453
f: +49 (0) 2234 205456
e: info@designeryarns.de
w: www.designeryarns.de

ICELAND
Storkurinn ehf
Laugavegi 59
101 Reykjavík
Iceland
t: +354 551 8258
f: +354 562 8252
e: storkurinn@simnet.is

SPAIN
Oyambre Needlework SL
Balmes, 200 At. 4
08006 Barcelona
Spain
t: +34 (0) 93 487 26 72
f: +34 (0) 93 218 66 94
e: info@oyambreonline.com

SWEDEN
Nysta garn och textil
Luntmakargatan 50
S-113 58 Stockholm
Sweden
t: +46 (0) 8 612 0330
e: nina@nysta.se
w: www.nysta.se

AUSTRALIA/NEW ZEALAND
Prestige Yarns Pty Ltd.
P.O. Box 39
Bulli
NSW 2516
Australia
t: +61 (0) 2 4285 6669
e: info@prestigeyarns.com
w: www.prestigeyarns.com

BRAZIL
Quatro Estacoes Com
Las Linhas e Acessorios Ltda
Av. Das Nacoes Unidas
12551-9 Andar
Cep 04578-000 Sao Paulo
Brazil
t: +55 11 3443 7736
e: cristina@4estacoeslas.com.br

MEXICO
Estambres Crochet SA de CV
Aaron Saenz 1891–7
Col. Santa Maria
Monterrey
N.L. 64650
Mexico
t: +52 (81) 8335 3870
e: abremer@redmundial.com.mx

For more information on my
other books and yarns, please
visit www.debbieblissonline.com

First published in the United States of America in 2008 by **Trafalgar Square Books** North Pomfret, Vermont 05053.

Printed in China

Originally published in the United Kingdom in 2008 by Quadrille Publishing Limited, London.

Text and project designs © 2008 Debbie Bliss Photography, design, and layout © 2008 Quadrille Publishing Limited

Library of Congress Control Number: 2008900778

ISBN: 978-1-57076-396-0

Editorial Director **Jane O'Shea**
Creative Director **Mary Evans**
Project Editor **Lisa Pendreigh**
Pattern Checker **Rosy Tucker**
Photographer **Ulla Nyeman**
Stylist **Julie Mansfield**
Illustrator **Kate Simunek**
Pattern Illustrator **Bridget Bodoano**
Production Director **Vincent Smith**
Production Controller **Ruth Deary**

10 9 8 7 6 5 4 3 2 1

First edition

acknowledgments

This book would not have been possible without the contribution of the following:

Jane O'Shea, Lisa Pendreigh, and **Mary Evans** at Quadrille Publishing who have been such an inspirational team to work with.

Julie Mansfield, the stylist, whose input, as always, has been invaluable.

Ulla Nyeman, for the simply beautiful photographs, and her assistants.

Sally Kvalheim, who did such a great job baby grooming.

And, of course, the fantastic kids: **AJ, Alfie, Angus, Carson, Elina, Erin, Femi, Iona, Jacob, LeiLei, Litzi, Shianne, Thomas, Tilda, Tilly,** and **Tirion.**

Rosy Tucker, not only for pattern checking but for her wonderful design and creative contribution.

Penny Hill, for her essential pattern compiling and organizing the knitters.

The knitters, for the huge effort they put into creating perfectly knitted garments under deadline pressure: **Cynthia Brent, Barbara Clapham, Pat Church, Pat Clack, Jacqui Dunt, Shirley Kennet, Maisie Lawrence,** and **Frances Wallace.**

My fantastic agent, **Heather Jeeves.**

The **distributors, agents, retailers,** and **knitters** who support all my books and yarns, and make all my projects possible.